Praise for

Unapologetic

"This isn't a book—it's a permission slip. A powerful, personal call to stop waiting for validation and start leading from the inside out. Cassy reminds us that authenticity isn't a buzzword—it's the blueprint for impact."

—RYAN ESTIS, keynote speaker, entrepreneur, and author of *Prepare for Impact*

"As a brand strategist, I've worked with countless powerhouse women—but Cassy Williamson is in a league of her own. She doesn't just tell her story; she hands you the courage to own yours. *Unapologetic* is a bold, beautiful invitation to rise, reclaim your voice, and choose joy no matter what you've walked through. Equal parts pep talks and purpose, this book reminds you that your light was never meant to be dimmed!"

—CAROLINE KALENTZOS, CEO at POSH PR® and Pretty Doll Beauty

"If you've ever been told to tone it down or change who you are—and knew deep down that wasn't the answer—this book is for you. In *Unapologetic,* Cassy Williamson breaks through the grip of others' control and false expectations, inviting you to live boldly and faithfully as the person God created you to be."

—RYAN TAFT, founder and CIO of Impact Eighty-Eight, author of *Story Getter* and *The Sales Cure*

"Raw, radiant, and relentlessly real—*Unapologetic* is a love letter to the parts of ourselves we were once told to silence. Cassy reminds us that our too-muchness is exactly what makes us magic."

—AMY DRUHOT, author of *Just Brave It*

"This isn't a feel-good book; it's a full reset. If you're someone who's built success by performing, *Unapologetic* gives you the strategy to stop shape-shifting and start living fully as yourself. Cassy is a true expert—part coach, part catalyst—and this book will change how you lead, work, and show up in every room. You don't need another pep talk; you need this book."

—ASHLEE NELSON, founder and CEO of Ashlee Nelson Curated Events

"In this book, Cassy challenges you to move beyond the 'in-between'—the space where doubt and delay linger. After reading *Unapologetic*, you'll realize that you were created to move forward, to rise up, and to make an impact—not as a watered-down version of yourself, but as the bold, authentic 'you' the world truly needs."

—CHELSEA TIMMONS, real estate thought leader and executive

"This book is the rally cry for anyone who's ever asked, 'Is it okay to want more?' *Unapologetic* answers with a resounding 'yes'—and then hands you the map to go get it. From page one, you're pulled into a journey that's both fierce and freeing. With warmth, wit, and unshakable conviction, Cassy helps you shake off the noise, rise into your calling, and show up for yourself like never before. Every chapter helps you rediscover your light and learn to stand in it—fully, fiercely, and without compromise. This isn't just a book you read—it's one you feel. A transformational invitation to remember who you are and boldly become who you're meant to be. You'll turn the last page forever changed."

—BROOKE JOCK, sales and marketing executive

"In *Unapologetic*, Cassy Williamson writes with the kind of fearless honesty that reminds us how boldness and kindness can coexist—a unique formula for charisma. As a new parent, I was especially moved by her invitation to raise kids who lead with confidence and stay true to their shine. Read this for a jolt of real talk, self-love, and unapologetic joy."

—MILAM MILLER, author of *The Charisma Craft* and founder of Be Confident and Kind

Cassy Williamson

Unapologetic

A Journey to
Living Boldly, Loving Fiercely,
and Being Nothing but Yourself

www.amplifypublishing.com

Unapologetic: A Journey to Living Boldly, Loving Fiercely, and Being Nothing but Yourself

For more information, please contact:
Amplify Publishing, an imprint of Amplify Publishing Group
620 Herndon Parkway, Suite 220
Herndon, VA 20170
info@amplifypublishing.com

Library of Congress Control Number: 2025909412
CPSIA Code: PRV0525A
ISBN-13: 979-8-89138-723-2

Printed in the United States

To that fourteen-year-old boy with blonde hair, blue eyes, the biggest heart, and the perfect butt for football pants—there isn't a day that I'm not grateful to call you my husband, my best friend, my baby daddy, and my greatest gift.

I have been made unapologetically me through your unwavering love and support.

I love you the most.

Contents

Part Three

Introduction

• • •

MY NAME IS CASSANDRA, but I go by Cassy. My name is almost always mispronounced as Casey, but if you're ever in question, know that I've been called Sassy Cassy a time or two—that normally does the trick.

A few things to know about me are that I have a big personality, a lot of energy, a strong drive, and a love to love on people.

What does that mean? Well, most of the time love from me comes in the form of hugs and arm pats. As I've gotten older, I will admit my growing attempt to "reel it in." I know not everyone wants to be hugged, I promise.

I have moved over 30 times in my life between six states, which has given me what many have called an "interesting" accent. I spent most of my time growing up in Illinois, but have always been a wannabe Southerner. I guess that's why I've spent most of the last decade in the South. In seventh grade, I went to show choir camp and spent a week sharing a room with three girls from Mississippi.

My parents said that when they picked me up, my accent was so thick they couldn't understand me. Of course that accent quickly faded, but much of what I learned from these girls stuck. I continue to call so many of these humans "my people" as they've represented places of comfort and home.

Although I talk WAY too fast to be truly *Southern*, I'm all about y'all. I don't know a stranger, I'm not afraid to slow down to learn someone's story, and I will take a long drive on a country road to clear my head. I'm sure someone from the South would argue there's a lot more to it than that, but I'm reminded every time I go back north to visit how much I love the warmth of where I live. I've adopted many Southern mannerisms and phrases because they speak to my heart (whether you're blessing it or not). I tend to overshare, overtalk, and overdo it, which I hope you'll feel and read throughout this book. I'm also very much that friend who uses too many exclamation points, overemphasizes messages, and sends GIFs to support my statements because it feels like that's the closest thing I can put in text that would match the "me" you'd meet.

I have a lot of "Cassy-isms," quote too many movies, and oftentimes get well-known phrases and sayings wrong. A quick example would be that I say "ducks in the pond" instead of "ducks in a row." Not sure where the mix-up occurred, but this just works better for me and as much as it drives my husband crazy, I'm sticking with it.

You'll likely read a few of these and I promise I'm well aware that they're not how the sayings go, but that's one of the perks of writing your own book. If you choose to write your own one day, I hope you write it exactly as you see fit too.

Life has shown up in more than a few crazy ways for me. Whenever things hit a new level of "crazy," traumatizing or even low…I'd always say (too lightheartedly) it's going in my book one day. You see, I've always been an oddball, outcast, uniquely me.

I've always been Unapologetic in how I show up, stand up, and represent. These probably sound like positive traits to most and it's something I love about myself now. But I also have a list of people out there who were subject to a fierceness that I wish I could go back and not tame, but refine.

You see, my presentation and delivery weren't always kind and poised. My responses were not always carefully thought out and considered. I'm not here to pretend I've done or said everything right because I definitely haven't. Being Unapologetically You doesn't mean that you're Unapologetic. It means that you're embracing your most authentic self by leaning into your purpose without compromise.

This requires a pretty hefty learning curve, and I know I've let down and hurt others along the way. I own the fact that I'm still a work in progress. I am especially grateful to those who saw the diamond in the rough early on and loved me through it all in light of my faults.

Since I can remember, I've been leading my own way. I'm a high energy, warm and fuzzy, against-the-grain kind of human who will wear you down with love and hugs (as I mentioned) if you let me. I believe with all my heart that life is too short to change or compromise who you were meant to be.

Over the last few years, I've felt more and more called to share my experiences in hopes of serving someone else's story. I've had one too many people tell me that for "someone like me" (me being referenced as "happy, energetic, excited, driven, motivational"), it's very surprising to learn about my *challenging* or *traumatic* history and despite hearing this reaction repeatedly, I still have never understood why.

Does "happy" mean you haven't been through hardships?

Despite my own confusion with this statement, my response is consistently the same. In life, we get to make choices. I've chosen to find the light. I look for the good. And I fight for my happiness. It's all a choice. So my hope and purpose in writing this book is that as you hop on the roller coaster ride that's been my life so far, you laugh, reflect, and feel driven to assess your own life and choose the happy things for yourself too.

When we choose joy, look for light, and seek out the good, we will live more fulfilling lives. You'll more easily be able to embrace your purpose, your "why," and your most Unapologetic Self. Whether you're a student, recent graduate, entering the workforce, walking away from your profession, changing jobs, growing your family, or trying to figure out what the heck to do next, I hope you're here because of a drive to be bigger, bolder, and louder.

I want this book to create a community, place, and tribe to be Unapologetic. Like me, you likely come with your own list of "tone it down" stories, trauma, hardships, and life lessons.

You've personally experienced compromising who you are, making yourself smaller, or sacrificing your "why" for a relationship, job, family, or environment that you found yourself in. But you don't want to stay there. If you did, you wouldn't be here with me. I believe you're here because you're looking for a place where you can not only relate, but find action.

We're not here because we want to set up shop in this place of "in between." We want direction on how to grow out of it.

With every ounce of me, I hope and pray that this book helps create that space for you. I hope it gives you the tribe, affirmation, and drive to take your next steps toward change…I hope you believe in your Unapologetic Self as much as I do because you're worth fighting for.

As I believe you're worth every bit of that fight, so are the people around you. I hope you'll reflect about those around you who are also embracing their Unapologetic Selves. What are you for them? Are you an encourager? A believer? How do you support the people in this community?

I think we can all agree that life has dealt us hard hands at one point or another, but no person's story is the same. For me, the "hard" became more than I could manage in sixth grade.

This is also uncoincidentally when my depression and anxiety took their real shape.

Up until that point, I felt like I did okay embracing who I was, finding friends, and managing my quirks. But when we transitioned to middle school, when girls got meaner, when life got harder, when kids had to start "clique-ing out," I started to lose myself. I began to lose my why and struggled with making it through each day. I found my survival in music, theater, and my teachers. I found safe haven in their classrooms and in spaces where I felt like I could Make a Difference as me, not what was "popular."

If you're a parent to a middle schooler, it's no secret that this is a challenging time. I'd argue that it's even tougher now because social media has created a space where we cannot simply "turn it off," ever. It's all-consuming, all the time. After my extremely challenging sixth grade year, my parents felt that moving schools was the solution to my problems.

Unfortunately, what I found was that the problems I attempted to avoid continued to follow me from school to school. I began to realize it wasn't a school problem but each school played an important part of my journey to being my Unapologetic Self. Where I wasn't being bullied by a peer, I found myself in conflict with a teacher, coach, and even principal. I share this with you because if you haven't experienced these hardships personally, it's imperative you recognize them in the world around you, if not for yourself, for someone near you who's struggling.

Too many people have been through similar situations in their academic journeys.

I didn't fit in the box, and without shame, I admit that I still don't. Do you find yourself forcing yourself into a box because it's easy? Comfortable? Predictable? I want my stories to challenge this perspective for you because if we're not uncomfortable, we're not growing. Period. If we're not growing, we're not excelling to our full potential.

Throughout middle school, high school, college, graduate school, and my career, I've stayed uncomfy.

Want to know what I've discovered? We can't learn the lessons life is trying to teach us without the experiences, adversity, and discomfort.

I wouldn't be writing this book for you right now. You have to lean into these corners of your life to truly grow, find your purpose, and be your Unapologetic Self.

As we conclude each chapter, you'll find what I've coined "Unapologetic Truths." The "Unapologetic Truths" are what we can call your homework, if you so choose. These lessons are meant to serve you and drive you forward. Whether it's a lesson you apply to your own life, pass along to someone you love, or challenge your viewpoint as a parent or leader, I encourage you to take off those blinders and be open to a new perspective. You can find a section for taking notes at the end of the book.

So as we embark on this journey together, I want to give you a bit of a road map so you know where we're headed. Part I lays the foundation for *Unapologetic*. Discover the roots of my mindset and self-discovery as I navigate the challenges, relationships, and lessons that shaped my early journey.

In Part II, explore the transformative power of hope, connection, and authenticity through the people, moments, and choices that brought light to even my darkest times.

Finally, in Part III, step boldly into growth, courage, and purpose by owning your story, leading with heart, and shining Unapologetically in every facet of your life.

Below, you'll find the truths and lessons you can expect to take away from each chapter. Some of you may read this book cover to cover, while others may jump around to the sections that speak to you most. Either way, my hope is that these truths resonate with you, inspire change, and leave a lasting impact—just as they have for me.

Part I:
Unapologetic Truth #1: Growing with Grace
Unapologetic Truth #2: Look to Leaders who Shape Us
Unapologetic Truth #3: The Right Lessons from the Wrong Turns
Unapologetic Truth #4: When Dreams take a Detour
Unapologetic Truth #5: The Future isn't Back There
Unapologetic Truth #6: Family Worth Fighting For
Unapologetic Truth #7: You are Not Alone

Part II:
Unapologetic Truth #8: Choose the Light
Unapologetic Truth #9: Exit to Elevate
Unapologetic Truth #10: The Power of Presence
Unapologetic Truth #11: Boldly Share Kindness
Unapologetic Truth #12: Connection Over Convenience
Unapologetic Truth #13: Impact Over Effort
Unapologetic Truth #14: Follow the Winks
Unapologetic Truth #15: Love and Live Now

Part III:
Unapologetic Truth #16: Rise Through Failure
Unapologetic Truth #17: Boundaries Build Bridges
Unapologetic Truth #18: Give Thanks for the Journey
Unapologetic Truth #19: The People You Keep
Unapologetic Truth #20: Unapologetically Parenting
Unapologetic Truth #21: An Ode to Dolly
Unapologetic Truth #22: More than Enough
Unapologetic Truth #23: Born to Stand Out
Unapologetic Truth #24: Purpose over Perfection
Unapologetic Truth #25: Boldly Beautiful

During my coaching sessions with current and emerging leaders, we often discuss that leadership without humility is lost. If we aren't willing to learn from everyone and everything around us, we're missing so many opportunities to grow. Whether those lessons are good or bad is irrelevant. A lesson is a lesson.

Through high school and college, my sister and I spent several years in the music industry speaking and singing under our band name "Chasing Hope." It was a platform we poured our hearts and souls into, primarily working with military kids. When it came to our music careers, it was honestly what we hoped we would "be" when we grew up. We believed that the music industry was lacking messages with a purpose serving our younger generation. Chasing Hope was meant to deliver music with messages that no one else was singing about.

More on that to come, but I share that with you as I want to end with the lyrics to our song "Make a Difference" as it serves as not only the foundation for the rest of the book, but a primary core value in my life. I want you to ask yourself now and throughout the book, "What is my purpose? Who do I want to serve?"

Whether you're already doing it, working toward your vision, or still finding your way, ask yourself, "Am I embracing my Unapologetic Self to work toward my life's purpose?" What can you do to make a difference? How can you change a life? Be a leader and a fighter. Make a difference, change a life.
— Chasing Hope

And just a quick disclaimer: One thing I know to be true, just like me, this book won't be everyone's cup of tea. It's not meant to be. It's here because if I can challenge you to challenge yourself, someone you love, or both, then sharing my story with you has served its purpose.

• • •

Part One

Chapter One

Back to School

• • •

I WAS IN SIXTH GRADE when bullying started to get really bad. I was small…so small that "Shortie" was what my few friends called me. When you get called *small* enough times, it's amazing how at 11 years old you start to act *small* too. Nevertheless, I generally loved school.

I had struggled in third grade with a horrible substitute teacher. Our amazing, wonderful teacher Mrs. M was on maternity leave and her fill-in fell way more than short.

This new teacher, Mrs. G., timed us in the bathroom, y'all, like punching a clock but for the facilities, and in third grade she felt like a real-life Miss Trunchbull that we were all convinced had a chokey hiding somewhere in the storage closet.

Fourth and fifth grade were in a completely new building and after Trunchbull it was nice to have a fresh start. I had friends, good teachers, and I made it through just fine. But as I moved toward middle school, I became visibly more awkward, odd, and different compared to my peers.

During this time, I leaned into music and theater, finding my voice on a stage. I'm still grateful to this day for Nancy, a local director, who saw light, love, and life in me far before so many others did.

Picture a puny, pale, dark-haired me with no mascara. Got the image? All right, now add a lot of dark clothing…I was depressed, y'all, and looking back I believe this is when my anxiety took on an entirely new shape. I had a full-blown **complex** going to school. Riding the bus, getting off the bus, the lockers, class transitions, and a new group of kids—it wrecked me.

I felt so lost and it was in sixth grade when the bullying started to get really bad. I was made fun of for anything you can think of. Sure there were the basics like my clothes, my size, and my looks, but then they just crossed the line. We were honoring a little boy with special needs in our class, whom I knew because I sat with him along with the rest of his class at lunch. I loved being around the energy, happiness, and pure joy these individuals shared.

This was before "inclusion" and I wanted to be around these kids. They were a light in my very dark school day. Not only did I get scrutinized for my lunch table choices, but when I got to sing over the intercom for him, I put an even bigger target on my back.

I know you may be reading this thinking "kids will be kids," "kids are ruthless," "kids are brutal," but what I've come to realize time and time again is that kids grow up to be grown-ups and these kids are now adults who dealt us some really awful behavior. At some point, even the good people break.

Outside of school, after a grueling audition process, I was chosen to be Annie at Springfield Theater Center. Remember the girl I described earlier; now add red hair to the mix. For some reason, my mom made the decision that dyeing my hair red and putting a perm in it would be a better route than a wig, because why not?

I did you the great service of finding the picture to enlighten you all. Two words: HOT MESS.

**pictured: Cassy (left) as orphan Annie and her sister (right) as orphan Molly*

I poured my heart into that show. The show was such a hit that we got to add an extra weekend…a dream come true for me. I can say wholeheartedly that being in that show carried me through that school year. The best part was that after each show, the entire cast and crew got to meet people from the audience.

There were so many little girls (much younger than me) who met me with this awe and excitement. We took pictures. I signed their programs and poured as much light and love into each of them as an 11-year-old could. It was the first time I felt like I was making a difference.

That feeling is something I still chase today. But as it always does, Monday reared its ugly head, and it was time to go back to school.

I had a few teachers who came to the show, who supported me, loved me, and saw things in me I couldn't. Mrs. Slater's room was a place I felt safe and knew I could run to. For her and the others, I am eternally grateful, but sixth grade could not be over soon enough.

I knew I was not the only target. This was a hard year for a lot of us, but one girl in particular my heart still hurts for. I so regret that in my "smallness," I didn't grow bigger to stand up for her.

I told y'all I have a list.

She wore the same clothes to school every day, didn't smell like a person who'd been given what all of us deserve for basic hygiene, and was also bigger than most kids in our class. When she walked through the halls, they shouted "Rhino, Rhino" at her, acting like the ground was shaking and making faces to follow suit.

I remember my heart breaking for her, but I was barely surviving myself. It's amazing how God can try to show you that you're not alone, but at 11 years old, believing that is a totally different story. I went back to hide in my own shadow.

When my family reflected back on that year, they often said I wasn't "me." I take their word for it as I've blocked out so much of it that it's hard for me to even recall. What I do remember feeling is that "Cassy" had been bullied or beaten out of me. But not to worry, she wouldn't be lost forever.

That was my last year in that school district thanks to another relocation. We moved houses on basically an annual basis. For the longest time, I always attributed it to my mom loving a good project. She was really talented at decorating, and I thought new houses were like a new adventure, so we moved…a lot.

Unapologetic Truth #1: Growing with Grace

As I've grown older, I think that moving from place to place for us was an escape. It was like running away, family edition. But what became very obvious after a few moves was that the place wasn't always the problem. In fact, the place rarely was. So although we moved homes, changed schools, and skipped town, the problems seemed to find us again and again. Why? Because the problem was about a person, not the place.

I still find this true as an adult and see it in my professional and personal experiences. Ever hear the saying, "It's not about where you are; it's who you're with"? This particular quote is meant to be interpreted in a way that suggests it's not the place, but the people who make an experience, and I agree.

On the flip side, what is also true is that just as the **right people** can make any "space," the same can be true about the **wrong people** disrupting even the ideal spaces.

Can you think of a time when you felt you were in the perfect job, neighborhood, school, or maybe even vacation, but a person or group of people tarnished that experience? I know I can.

In sixth grade I was confused, lonely, and lost. I thought that my school was the problem, but what I'd later discover is that even in a new school, with new people, the problems didn't disappear. I was still me.

So what's the solution? How do we evoke change? How do we Make a Difference in not only our own lives, but the lives of the next generation?

We can't keep running, avoiding, or ignoring. This also isn't time for the blame game. It's actually quite the opposite. The solution here that we desperately lack isn't rocket science. It's simply *grace*. And that's where we have to start. Fighting for it, giving it, teaching it, and believing in it.

Life is hard enough without human disruptors. And although I don't see bullying or ugly people magically disappearing any time soon (a girl can dream though, right?), I want us to reflect on what we're doing to empower ourselves, our friends, and our kids.

Almost 20 years later and not much has changed from when I was in sixth grade. Adults turn their heads away from anything uncomfortable and kids do too. Do you?

Take a moment to reflect on these questions.

- What am I modeling?
- How am I responding to what's different around me?
- Do I embrace the people around me who are Unapologetically themselves?
- If not, why?

I think the answer to a lot of our problems starts with grace. If we had it, showed it, embraced it, the world would be a much more forgiving, welcoming place. The first step to being Unapologetic is to give yourself grace and then show it too.

• • •

Chapter Two

Small School, Big Problems

• • •

IN SEVENTH GRADE, I moved to a small, private Christian school and was hopeful that this fresh start would be my ticket. This would be the path that led to me fitting in and being Unapologetically Me without backlash. I hadn't yet realized what we just discussed.

This school was **small**. To paint a picture, my sister and I were four doors down from each other while she was in third grade and I was in "middle school."

Everyone was in the same two halls with the exception of the few classes the seventh and eighth graders had upstairs. I can still picture our principal riding through the halls on her electric scooter.

I really thought I would find my place here. I was so excited and eager for a fresh start. The reality though was I'd just found an even smaller space to stand out in a place where our principal wanted us all to "get in line."

I joined the student council and had the greatest mentor, Mrs. M. I also met some of the very first influential friends I'd ever have. These friendships gave me my first glimpse into what felt like a "normal" childhood and built a foundation for relationships I just hadn't had.

We had slumber parties, fashion shows, and photo shoots and made up silly dance routines. We rode four-wheelers, went on adventures, and frequented the movies and skating rink. It was an absolute blast, and I cherish those memories.

At school, my friends and I became quick targets of inappropriate scrutiny from our elderly principal. As part of the student council, we were tasked with raising money for various events like school dances.

In a school as small as ours, we had to get creative to make money; a lemonade stand wasn't going to cut it. Lucky for us, the student council obtained approval to host "Dollar Fridays" where students could pay a dollar to dress in jeans and a shirt. That's right; in private school you paid to dress in clothes of your choice. Crazy, I know.

If it wasn't a dollar day, we were wearing approved pants and a "uniformed" polo. Keep in mind that this was the early 2000s, so if you're too young, t-shirts and jeans paired with two to four layers of colored camis under your shirt was THE cool thing. The only chance or shot you had at exemplifying *style* was on dollar days.

This was also when Hollister and Abercrombie were all the rage, but my mom was not going to pay for me to wear those brands, so it was up to me to pay for these clothes if I wanted them.

Even as a preteen I was stubborn and determined. I'd save everything I could, get to the mall, and head right to the clearance rack because the only thing a 12-year-old me could afford was the $12.90 Hollister t-shirt.

Anything else was out of the question. But as long as I was wearing "Hollister," who cared what rack it came from? I was so proud of these three, maybe four, t-shirts I had because I went totally broke to buy them.

I never could have imagined the agony and anguish these t-shirts would create.

It was Dollar Friday, and I was proudly wearing one of my new shirts when my principal pulled me into the hall.

Keep in mind, I'm twelve, wearing a t-shirt and jeans with what I still called "mosquito bites" for body parts. If you're still not tracking, I was wearing a bra, but only because it was built into my camisole, not because I had much of anything up there.

I'm standing in the hall when my principal begins lecturing me about my appearance and values. She goes on to accuse me of attracting the wrong kind of attention (on purpose), stating that my t-shirt is far too tight. She concludes this grand lecture with a line about how inappropriate this attire is for school and Jesus.

Oof. I went from feeling like a proud entrepreneur to being covered by a wave of shame and embarrassment. I can't tell you if I cried in front of her or not, but I felt so small. I was being condemned by someone whose role was to lead, encourage, and empower.

I fully recognize certain situations warrant direction, guidance, and constructive criticism, but I assure you, this was not that moment.

These moments, accusations, and scrutiny continued for me and my closest friends. We were classified as troublemakers, a problem class, disrespectful, and rebellious.

In eighth grade, we were put through an abstinence class that was taught separately for the guys and the girls. Although

I didn't have the opportunity to attend the guys' version of the class, I do know that they weren't referred to as human "plants" who should "protect their flowers at all cost." Again, bizarre.

The school's attempt to restrict and confine us only drove us (or most of us) further away. What should have been lighthearted moments and events of adolescence became illogically censored. School dances consisted of filtered playlists and parent chaperones patrolling the dance floor demanding we leave "room for Jesus" with every move.

I'm not sure how you picture your Jesus, but we left enough room for Jesus and all 12 of his apostles.

On field trips, their extremely strict dress codes followed us even into the water park. Too bad for them, snowsuits were not waterslide capable.

I can only laugh at it now because it was so backward. They really believed that by sheltering us and keeping us completely "covered" physically that they'd keep us from doing what most normal, hormonal preteens would do. The plan only backfired.

Seeing that this was my first time in a private school along with my first real experience in the Christian church, I struggled with where God was in all of this. How could this be the place that claimed to represent the love of Jesus?

As a mom myself I recognize that we have to protect our kids, but consider the boundary between protection and restriction. What we were experiencing was not a form of "loving" protection.

I had gone from a school filled with mean and hateful students to one with mean and hateful adults. I'll let you come to your own conclusions on which you think is worse.

> Although we were probably one of the more challenging classes they'd had, I think my joining our already small class completely rocked the boat. The principal might as well have called me Ren in her version of *Footloose*.

Who knew that the makeup-wearing, hoops-loving (that's earrings y'all, not basketball), Hollister-t-shirt-buying "wild" child could cause so many problems? What that principal failed to capture was who I was underneath what she chose to see, and that's the point.

Two long years later, my class was finally closing the door on a very odd middle school experience. Fortunately, the diversity had bonded us and we ended our time together on a happy, high note.

After a lengthy approval process initiated by my music teacher, I got to sing "Who Am I" by Casting Crowns at our graduation ceremony. This was only because no one had yet written "Room for Jesus on the Dance Floor," which would have been my first selection. ☺

Jokes aside, our small class celebrated together in every way possible before heading off to high school. I'd found my voice again and was genuinely looking forward to our next chapter, high school.

Unapologetic Truth #2: Look to Leaders who Shape Us

This one is a bit different and actually two-fold.

1. There will be people in our lives who *should* be in our corner, have our best interests in mind, and operate to see us succeed. As kids, most would agree that these would be parents, family members, educators, coaches, and so on.

We expect more from these individuals because we were raised to think that they would look out for us. But the harsh reality is that this cannot be the assumption, and it is most definitely not always the case. So how do we support our youth in protecting their voices and themselves in these spaces and situations? How do we help them prepare for the people who will only see them as they choose to see them?

Not everyone has the support at home to know the "right" from the "wrong." Few are even fortunate enough to have people advocating for them when the education system doesn't. So although I don't have the answer on how to solve this massive problem, I do believe that an opportunity we have in our journey to find this solution starts for many of us at home.

Are we having open and honest conversations with our kids? Are we empowering them to talk to us about even the uncomfortable moments? Do they know that we trust them, hear them, and support them no matter what?

I was fortunate to be able to talk to my parents about what was going on at school and so were my friends. Solutions to many of the occurrences happening at school were resolved quickly by our parents advocating for us.

I fully acknowledge that we can't repair something we didn't break. But we can empower our kids to know when to tag us in. It's essential that we create a space and an environment that allows them that opportunity. I believe this is the first small step toward change.

2. If you're reading this as a person in a position of influence, especially with younger adolescents, I would challenge you to reflect on your own interactions.
    - What kind of language do you use with these kids?
    - How do you show them that you see AND hear them?
    - What example are you setting in your actions?
    - How are you supporting (if at all) their journey to finding their voice, purpose, and Unapologetic Self?

I don't think that our school's leadership had awareness of the negative impacts their behavior was having on each of us. I want to believe that they felt like they were doing what was best for us. However, even after conflicts were confronted, they continued to disregard the weight of their words, actions, and strategy in a space where they should've been supporting our education and development.

So whether you're a parent or a person of influence to our littles (or not-so-littles), I would consider the power you have to shape our next generation. Our kids need support, love, and empowerment. They're looking to us for guidance, reassurance, and leadership. Be a person they remember years from now as someone who lifted them, inspired them, and celebrated who they were aspiring to be.

• • •

Chapter Three

Fourteen

• • •

DON'T ASK ME WHY OR HOW, but on the first day of what should've been my freshman year, my dad and I were sitting in the administrative office of my planned high school being denied a transfer request that we thought we'd had approved all summer.

I still to this day don't understand how we got to the first day of school without figuring this out sooner, but that's just something I've chosen not to dwell on. Either way, I was left with either the public school I was zoned for (my previous sixth grade district) or I'd have to start another new private school journey with the Catholic school.

Reflecting back, I'm just not sure how they said "no" to my dad. I mean I did all the time, but how could they? He made a strong case and what was one more admission? But there we were with a big fat, "Sorry, there's nothing else we can do."

It's so funny how things can blow up, not work out, and go completely sideways for the most perfect of reasons. Of course, we never have a clue in the moment, and this was very much the case here too. I had no idea at the time that God was leading me into what would become the hardest chapter of my life while also guiding me to the person who would save it too.

And there on the first day of school, I found myself sitting with my dad in the principal's office of the private school 10 minutes away completing registration for what would now be my freshman year at the private Catholic school. This was not the plan.

This was not the plan, the place, or the group of people I had "signed up for." This was the plot twist of **all** plot twists. My immature, emotional, dramatic, 14-year-old self was completely spiraling. I finally had friends and they'd be across town in the school we were supposed to go to together.

So where the heck do I go from here?

My first week at this school was like spending the entire summer at the kiddie pool and then on the very last day being thrown into the deep end without a floatie.

Y'all, they aren't kidding when they say the wild kids go to Catholic school. I say that with as much love in my heart as I can, but I all but came out from under my rock of conservative sheltering when I was **slapped** in the face with my freshman class.

I was exposed to a new world and although it wasn't all bad, it definitely wasn't all good either. I'll coin the name "Kissing Cassy" for myself because it's better for me to acknowledge it on my own terms here. I loved boy(s). Ironically, that plural would take a really **hard**, abrupt stop very soon.

I made friends, I had boyfriends, I embraced the high school experience. But more importantly, I was determined to fit in and at whatever cost. So I did, until I didn't. The ugliness that took shape the spring of my freshman year was right out of a scene from *Mean Girls*.

Similar to most 14-year-old girls, my friend circle all blew up over a boy. This particular boy wasn't one I was willing to go down fighting for—that boy will come later. This guy was just an ass. So I lost my only close friend and was quickly made an outcast.

She was far cooler than I was at the time and had gone to school with most of our class her entire life. I would've chosen her side too, but only because it was a lot easier that way. So there I was back on the bench, waiting for a friend.

In our class, there was a group of girls who hung in the middle…they stayed within everyone's good graces, didn't push the bar, and always had a place to sit at lunch. They played it safe, something I wish I felt called to do. I didn't then and I still don't. But either way, they were nice to me, and I was thankful.

One of them had a crush on a boy in our class whom I'd never met. She wasn't as outspoken as I was so what do you do for your friends who like a boy? You talk to him for them. I remember it (and him) like it was yesterday. We were in the hall outside of English class when I walked right up to this tall, blonde-haired, blue-eyed boy named Eric.

He was as cute as can be, but so quiet—like "talking to that poster in your room that isn't giving anything in return" quiet. Either way it didn't take long before Eric and my friend were "talking."

For those of you who are young, this was what we called it "back in the day." They weren't dating but they also weren't talking to other people. I won't share their story because that's not why we're here. What I will share is that it didn't work out between the two of them, and for that I am forever grateful.

It was the summer of 2007 when that same beautiful boy, Eric, and I started talking. On June 1, 2007, sitting on a barstool in his parents' basement, Eric officially asked me to be his girlfriend. That day will forever be one of my favorites. Those two 14-year-olds had no idea what life was about to hand them, but they had each other and didn't seem to need much else.

We had the most magical summer. That is, for two kids who couldn't drive, had no money, and spent most of their time outside. But even now, I still consider it magical. We had nothing and everything all at the same time. Just like that, I fell head over heels for Eric.

He made me laugh, he felt like home, and he showed me the kind of patience and grace that changed my entire life. His grandma referred to us as "puppy love," which back then really had the sassy Cassy in me feeling some sort of way, but can you imagine seeing us at 14? As an adult, I probably would've said the same thing too.

It wasn't until school started back in August that our relationship would be tested and challenged in ways neither of us could have imagined. School, of course, had always housed my worst days, but I never had an "Eric" by my side before.

In the midst of *Mean Girl* madness, Eric was my constant. He wrote me notes, walked me to class, and waited for me anywhere I went. He knew I struggled at school, but he didn't care. He was loyal and loving to a fault, still is.

Eric played football and got all kinds of crap from the team about dating me. He was unfazed. On weekends, he was rarely at parties because we were hanging out with his family. During the week, when he wasn't practicing and I wasn't working, we spent as much time out of school together.

We caught rides home together, visited with family, shared any meals we could, and I helped him with his homework, followed by more "homework"…sorry, Dad.

But really, I was too type A to not get good grades and I wanted Eric to do well too. I'm not sure what his GPA rose to after our first year of dating, but his mom definitely does. I'm going to pause here on Eric and me because although I could talk about him all day, our story is only just beginning.

Friends came and went for me as I moved through the year. Like most teenagers, I was desperately trying to find my place. For me, my escape had always been music and theater. That was only because I knew early on that I had no place on anything with the word "field" in it.

Too many strangers and friends alike have witnessed me tripping, falling, walking into a wall (that's always been there), or whacking myself accidentally with something. I don't pair well with coordination, so I've always known I'd be headed nowhere athletic.

Thankfully, my new high school was known for their theater program, music department, and accessibility to private voice and piano lessons. I was hoping to find my fit somewhere in that mix.

Unfortunately, I was not what you'd describe as a choir girl. I sang like I talk—**loud**—and my voice was in no way classically trained or inspired. I grew up singing Motown and oldies and it showed. My choir teacher at the time would also agree.

I was tolerated, but not lifted, led, challenged, or empowered. If anything, it was the opposite. After several months in the program, my choir teacher directly asked me not to sing in my "Cassy voice." It was devastating. What other voice was I supposed to sing in besides my own? Forced to tone it down, again.

I stuck with it for a while, but eventually walked away. I would use my voice, exactly as it was, singing with my sister as I had been my whole life. The craziest thing was that the school would later use my sister's and my music platform to recruit, despite their behavior while I was in attendance.

Unapologetic Truth #3: The Right Lessons from the Wrong Turns

I refer to 14 as THE year. This was the year that the trajectory of my life was forever changed. I had no idea the significance of every stop sign, detour, and unexpected transition during the course of this year. You'll soon learn more about my family, my relationships, and our journey with music.

But what I know now is that every single moment was leading me to exactly where I needed to be. Can you recall a time like this in your own life?

For many of us, it may take years before we're able to acknowledge or identify this in our own lives. When you're in the thick of it, you're more than likely going to be blinded by the storm. I personally was throwing a full-on pity party and questioning my "why" time and time again. Going through it oftentimes felt like a sick joke.

The inconsistencies at home, revolving friendships, and bullying at school were challenging, confusing, and defeating.

I felt like so much of an outcast in a space where I was hell-bent on fitting in. I just wanted to belong. Don't we all?

I learned so much about who I did and didn't want to be at 14. But my greatest lessons from this year didn't come until much, much later.

Isn't it funny how that works?

In the face of adversity, we are truly tested. Our character, strength, and faith. But it's critical to not lose sight of who we are and who we're meant to be in those moments.

I also think being Unapologetic as a teenager is far more challenging than as an adult. You're looking for your place and purpose while simultaneously navigating the challenges of school. Kids now are also forced into an online, on-demand culture, making it even easier to get wrapped up in what we think the world and people around us want us to be.

It makes more sense to compromise.

I wish that I'd found my sense of self and security much sooner in life. At 14, I was just scratching the surface. What I'm humbly willing to admit is that I'm still learning from every experience. And I would challenge you to open yourself up to the same.

How can we learn from not only the people around us, but the past versions of ourselves? We often say, "people don't change," or that people *can't* change. And maybe that's true to an extent. But we can evolve, grow, learn, and progress.

What was your moment, year, or plot twist?

Have you had it?

Is there something from that experience that can still grow and shape you now?

We're never too old to learn and that's the beauty of it.

• • •

Chapter Four

Chasing Hope

• • •

I HAVE ONE SISTER and we're three and a half years apart. Growing up, we were often pitted against one another. Everything was a competition. If we weren't being stacked against one another, we were having to choose sides in whatever fight was taking place that day, and choosing each other was not an option.

The competition and comparison war led to what felt like a lifelong saga that neither of us knew how to get through. But, by the grace of God (for real), we've reached the healthiest version of our relationship in the last two years.

Life has thrown us all sorts of curveballs, but our relationship has evolved and persevered through it all. We both have been extremely fortunate to find success in careers and our own families. We are raising our kids together and she will be one of the first people to read this book.

When any relationship is given such an unfair start, it will always have its own unique set of twists and turns. In spite of this, one thing has remained true: We always fought for each other too. In *true* big sister fashion, I can't think of a single person I wouldn't go up against to protect her. Then, now, and always.

For me, it's safe to say that no one knows or understands why I am the way I am like she does. It's also a rarity that a normal person could wrap their mind around what we've been through. So when things get heavy, we lean into that history, the unspoken bond, and push each other through.

We were raised weird, y'all. I'll admit that is the nicest possible word I can use so we're going to stick with that. The things that we were told, shown, and taught are still so bizarre to me. Our experiences were oftentimes traumatic, manipulative, and abusive.

Isolation from extended family was used as the master strategy so that we could be better controlled by the narrative. As we grew up, we didn't know what we didn't know. I was invested in and adored the wrong people.

I share this because our upbringing has a **lot** to do with why I have a full-on complex about the most random things. It fed my anxiety, insecurities, and confidence in the very worst way. If there was something to manipulate, we'd hear a bizarre story about a similar topic or incident. As an adult, I still can't delineate what was fable or fiction.

What I do know to be true is that I am extremely grateful that social media and video wasn't so streamlined yet. Our family likely would've gone viral, and not in a way I'd want to remember.

I often applaud myself as an adult in the most random of moments only because I **know** how far I've come. Working through your childhood's crazy BS is worthy of a celebration. Especially if it's taken you close to a decade's worth of counseling to get there.

I'm sharing this with you because it's okay to admit this. As I've grown, many of my own realizations were learned through embarrassing myself first. I've responded or reacted in a way that on the surface likely didn't make sense.

My responses often went a lot deeper than what meets the eye. I think that can be true for so many of us. Just like that saying, "Don't judge a person unless you've walked a mile in their shoes."

Basically, it's a Christmas miracle that both my sister and I made it "out" and "up." Period. We aren't perfect, we've definitely got our quirks, and we challenge our own "crazy" daily, but we don't deny it either and I definitely don't try to be something I'm not.

Despite the challenges of our childhood, music has been the magic that bonds us for life.

You have to know that my sister has more talent than most people could ever dream of. She could sing the roof off any arena if she chose to and at 11 years old was singing "Independence Day" as good as Martina McBride with half the effort. But, like my dad, she shies away from sharing this, so I'll gladly do it for her. We have always loved to sing and most days preferred to do it together.

We grew up singing anywhere they'd let us and by my mom's request for anyone who'd listen. There were some really good concerts at our grocery store and local nursing homes, let me tell you. As we grew older, we thought we could make a career out of it and we gave it all we had or at least all we could as two kids.

At the age of only 12, my sister wrote "The Price of Peace," which launched our music career. The song was written about a daughter's experience throughout her dad's deployment, to serve tribute to our military families.

This song would go on to be sponsored by State Farm Insurance and then later the National Guard. It was the platform we built our brand on and although it allowed us to impact this fantastic community of military kids, families, and supporting organizations, nothing could compare to the lasting impact it would have on our lives.

What began as a few opportunities to sing the song at local events grew into performing on a national platform. We had the opportunity to perform in spaces with Lee Greenwood, the Lt. Dan Band, and Eric Church.

We met some of the greatest military kids, influential military leaders, and organizations that were leading the charge for change advocating for our military families.

I developed a program called "Free to Rise Up" in an effort to serve bullying prevention, suicide awareness, and leadership initiatives among this population. We performed concerts at summer camps and arenas. We spoke and trained at leadership conferences and joint-readiness initiatives.

We were also exposed to real hardships, things that you didn't see on the news or hear people talking about. I'll never forget sitting across the table from a girl whose dad was blown up by an IED (improvised explosive device) and lived to tell the tale. Listening to her story and then his was one that would make a "normal" person question what they truly have to complain about.

We grew close to kids who lost their siblings or parents to war. We sang a song about coming home to units where not everyone got to come home. We cried and mourned with these families from all over the country.

Those moments live with you, change you, and provide a perspective like no other. It's impossible not to carry them with you for the rest of your life.

After almost five years, 27 states, and more life-changing experiences than we could've ever asked for, we chose to walk away. Through a challenging medical diagnosis, our parents' divorce, high school, college, and a lot of family drama in between, the magic had faded and the writing for Chasing Hope was on the wall.

With each event, we both grew more tired of the grind. Being in school full time, fighting within our family regularly, and giving those kids all we had when we were with them was taxing on us both. Neither of us has an ounce of regret about that time. I know that we did exactly what we were supposed to.

The kids that we met, the families whose testimonies we got to share, and the opportunities to challenge the narrative for military families was and still is one of my proudest accomplishments. We made a difference to those we were meant to serve, and it was the end of only a chapter, not our whole story.

Now, we will sing you a song when you ask us, but most concerts these days are held in our kitchen with our kids and I'm okay with that. God just had other plans. What we gained from those experiences and how we've grown together is what I'm most grateful for.

Unapologetic Truth #4:
When Dreams take a Detour

It's still a hard pill to swallow that my sister and I didn't make it "as planned" with our music career. We gave what felt like an entire lifetime to chasing that dream (or Chasing Hope) and our family as a whole made so many sacrifices along the way.

It was a painful journey for a lot of reasons and although that time was a gift and by no means wasted, it's always hard to face defeat, especially when it concerns a dream.

This is a lesson I remind myself often, as I think it's extremely important to recognize that the dreams we have for ourselves may not always match the big picture. The "big dream" may actually be only a part of your journey on the way to fulfilling your purpose.

My advice to you is to chase your dreams in only the biggest of ways, but be flexible in the journey. Be intentional in looking for the open doors, detours, and signs along the way. I'm a walking postcard for someone whose plan has **yet** to turn out the way I thought it would.

Keep these things in mind on your own journey:

* Find your voice and don't be afraid to use it.
* Lean into being Unapologetic.
* Be careful not to stand in your own way.
* Be open to the simple fact that God's plan is bigger than our own.
* Protect your heart, mental health, and family at all costs.
* Set the boundaries necessary to continue growing into the very best version of yourself.

As Kenny Rogers famously sang in "The Gambler," wisdom often comes down to knowing when to stay the course and when to step away.

Things won't always work out the way you hoped, I guarantee it, but it's like that old proverb, "Make plans and God laughs." On most days I feel like I'm probably a headliner for Heaven who keeps everyone on their toes and of course, laughing.

• • •

Chapter Five

Family to a Fault

• • •

AS I'VE SHARED, I was 14 when I started dating Eric. The pivotal year. This was the same year that things started to crash down around me at home. This is no coincidence, I promise. At that time, my parents were still married, my sister and I were actively chasing our dreams of a music career, my dad was active duty with the Army National Guard, and my mom owned her own business. On the outside, we looked like the perfect family.

You know what they say: Looks can be deceiving. My family situation could honestly be an entire book in itself and I wouldn't be surprised if there were people out there flipping open to **only** this section to see what I planned on sharing. Hate to disappoint any of the noseys, but this section is meant only to serve, just like the rest of the book, not throw shade.

So back to 2007…

My mom's business was a place entirely dedicated to all things fun for little girls. We had a storefront, hosted birthday parties, and gave makeovers to girls of all ages.

Both my sister and I helped at the store, and we spent a great deal of time there as a family, just like anyone else who owns their own business. My dad was doing work over the weekend and when changing one of the lights, he was electrocuted, triggering his onset of Parkinson's disease (PD).

We had no idea at the time that the small tremor that started in his right index finger would turn into a lifetime diagnosis, but at only 38 years old and several different neurologists later, he was given the definitive diagnosis.

It was shortly after receiving this diagnosis that my parents made the difficult decision to shut the doors of their business. This also meant that my mom had to walk away from her dream in an effort to shift her focus to my dad's health.

The challenge with this for my family was that we all grieve extremely differently. Although my mom had blown through the "acceptance" phase of grief and right into fix-it mode, my dad was most definitely not on the same page. For him, this diagnosis meant a lot more than walking away from our business.

So on top of a ridiculously heavy diagnosis and shutting the doors to our business, from my perspective, my parents' marriage began to crumble before my sister and me. It would be another six years before they actually got divorced.

I've got to take a moment for a random sidebar because it's too important not to. I'm not a counselor or a therapist and I'm not trying to be. What I am is the product of a very broken family.

My hope in sharing this with you is that it provides you a different perspective, one from the lens of the child. IF you are a parent who finds yourself sitting in an unhappy marriage (or relationship), hanging on for dear life for the sake of your kids, please consider this: Staying is not always the answer.

Staying in a toxic environment is not your only option, especially when you've exhausted what feels like ALL of the options.

My parents fought our entire life, they attempted a counseling appointment or two with no change, and they lost countless relationships with both friends and family through the process. It's admirable to make such a sacrifice for your family and kids, but at what cost? Life is too dang short.

My parents made a lot of sacrifices for my sister and me. Honestly, most of their marriage was a sacrifice. They did everything they could to make sure we had what we needed. They empowered us to chase after our dreams with everything we had and always did so right alongside us.

But on the other end of that were just two humans. Looking back, I see two imperfect people, like the rest of us, suffering from their own trauma, demons, and challenges with mental health, with little actually dealt with.

So what did this translate to for my sister and me? From my perspective, the expectation for perfection. We had to look absolutely perfect on the outside to everyone around us, all the time. We had to live up to the most unrealistic standards, knowing that nothing would actually ever be good enough. And we were expected to put our "good hats" on and pretend like we had it together, until we didn't.

If you've ever heard the quote, "You never know what people are going through. Sometimes the people with the biggest smiles are struggling the most, so be kind," let me just say: Nail. on. the. freakin'. head.

If I wasn't ever going to be good enough at home, I was going to do anything I could to make the people around me feel "good enough." At least they might have a chance.

As I've grown older, gone through counseling, and worked through my own demons, I've realized that a lot of my trauma is a result of generational trauma. My mom came from an extremely dark upbringing and my dad's was far from perfect as well.

Is this an excuse? No, but I share this because I want to believe my parents did their very best. I think this can be said for a lot of us. The problem is that trauma and its impact on your mental health are rarely battles you can (or should) fight on your own.

Unapologetic Truth #5: The Future isn't Back There

What a lot of counseling, Jesus, and consistent accountability from Eric has taught me is that boundaries are the only way we can change, transform, and grow. People are not always what they seem. Just because you "made it out" doesn't mean you're miraculously healed. We're not perfect; no one is.

The last thing I will say to so many who've struggled is that childhood trauma, if not dealt with as an adult, will continue to infiltrate your family for generations to come. It takes a lot of courage, effort, and hard work to break the cycle, but you're worth it, if not just for you, but for the people who love you too.

The biggest obstacle for me was accepting that a bloodline doesn't give you a get-out-of-jail-free card in life. Having a family tie doesn't mean you're allowed to do or say whatever you like indefinitely and expect unlimited forgiveness. When boundaries are crossed repeatedly, when you're denied respect continuously, and often left to be manipulated, then it's only YOU who can make the hard choices and either accept the behavior or walk away.

I've had to walk away from a lot of spaces and people that no longer served me. It's not easy, it doesn't go without heartache, but it is a decision that I made and will continue to make for not only myself but also for my marriage and my girls. If we don't set an example for them, who will?

For so long, I tried to minimize my own trauma by brushing it off because I held this belief that someone is always or has faced far worse than I have so who am I to complain? Have you found yourself in a similar position?

I haven't met a person yet who doesn't have a past, a history, or a story to share. Have you? We've all experienced hardships to some degree. Some of us are willing to share and some are not. Whether you know what a person's story is or not isn't relevant to you. What is important and essential in your journey is the belief that we all get to choose what kind of life we'll have in spite of what has happened to us. Consider this with me.

We can choose the "dark" or we can choose the "light." We can choose to allow the negative things happening around us or *to us* to consume us or we can choose to find the light in the darker or more challenging moments. Of course, both pose their own challenges, I won't sit here and pretend that it's easy, but one of these choices comes with a much greater reward.

My challenge for you is to choose the hard fight, the road less traveled, the tougher of the two options. I hope to encourage you to not only find the light, but be the light by shining your personal light. Some days it'll be easy and some days you'd honestly rather do anything else. Trust me, I feel you, I see you. I'm a work in progress too.

But the important thing to remember is that with a new day comes a new beginning, so don't take it for granted. We're not guaranteed anything in life, so I hope you choose the light.

• • •

Chapter Six

The Williamsons

• • •

WHEN I'M TALKING ABOUT ERIC and my story, I share that God knew exactly what he was doing when he gifted me with Eric at 14. I don't choose the word *gifted* lightly either.

Don't get me wrong, Eric and I have had our moments (lots of moments), but at a time when I couldn't seem to find the community I was desperately looking for at home, at school, or in music, I found it in what would become the greatest gift I've ever been given, the Williamsons. The timing was no coincidence—they would be the ones to save me.

Before I decided if I would share this part of my story or not, I put it in the hands of one of the most beautiful people on the planet, my mother-in-law, Michelle. Much of what I have to share is both their story and mine so when I was given her blessing, I knew that it was something I couldn't leave out.

Prior to meeting the Williamsons, Eric had told his family that he'd met "the most amazing girl in the world" and as a kid who didn't say much, he really set the bar high for me on that one. I wasn't nervous, but I knew the stakes were high.

Eric displayed a great deal of pride about his family, and I knew they were close without his needing to tell me so. I remember walking into their house for the first time and just feeling the warmth, welcome, and love that resonated there. I met Michelle and immediately knew that I was home.

At the time, I was embracing what I'll nicely call a "hippie phase," wearing homemade hemp necklaces, a peace sign (or a few), and a tie-dyed shirt that I still look back at and laugh. We are never as cool as we thought we were.

> Luckily for me, I quickly learned that I could've been wearing Ralphie's bunny suit while delivering the stockinged leg lamp from *A Christmas Story* (you know the one?) and Michelle would've still welcomed me with open arms.

To describe her as best as I can, Michelle gives most people a run for their money…in all the ways. Although no relationship or person is perfect, she's the best example of unconditional love I could ever think of. We couldn't find a dark tunnel that she can't find the light in or a person she can't find grace for.

She will find joy in any situation she can and laughs more over dinner than most people do all day. Michelle always has room for one more at her table and we love her so much for that. That summer she took me in and from that point forward would be a pillar in my life; I just didn't know it yet.

Almost two decades later, the Williamsons are still what I call the *Leave It to Beaver* family. They genuinely like each other, y'all. They don't love each other just because they have to; they enjoy being around one another.

Eric was one of four boys and their house was a home. They had both sets of grandparents actively involved in their life. They came to their sporting events and have always been there cheering them on from whatever "stand." During the holidays, the entire family would get together, with aunts, uncles, and cousins too.

> And it never felt like *National Lampoon's Christmas Vacation* either. Sure, they've got a quirky Cousin Eddie or two, but these gatherings were filled with love, laughs, and home videos. I know this may be hard for you to imagine, trust me; I wouldn't believe it either if not for seeing it.

Before the Williamsons, I spent most of my holidays sitting alone at the table stubbornly avoiding eating ham because my mom wasn't going to give up a power trip and I wasn't going to eat something that looked like scabs on the outside. I blame my sensory issues. Being invited to these gatherings was the gift; anything else (like eating what I wanted) was just a bonus.

The greatest piece of all of this was that Michelle and Eric's dad, Greg, were and are both tremendous examples of not only parents, but partners too. Being around them is still like getting to be inside of the snow globe, not just something you admire from the outside. Much like the snow globe, you almost always feel happier after being around them.

I took advantage of any opportunity I had to be with the Williamsons. My biological grandparents weren't allowed to be around us growing up (add it to the list), so Eric's grandparents quickly became mine. They opened their arms to me in a way that most wouldn't to the 14-year-old girlfriend. They gave me back some of the pieces of my brokenness and showed me a new kind of family, what family should and could be.

We were never doing anything fancy, and that was the best part. Enjoying meals together, watching movies, seeing Eric play football, or traveling to the grandparents' houses…it all just felt like magic to the kid coming from a family of four.

I eventually traveled with them for vacation and quickly learned a whole lot about the Williamson road trip structure. I'm not sure about y'all, but we were only allowed **one** stop in my family. We used the bathroom, got gas, and ate all at the same place. The Williamsons, on the other hand, made **several** pit stops. Michelle would say it's about the journey, not the destination, or something like that. ☺ They're worth it.

Through long distance, a nasty breakup, divorce, illness, death, and everything in between, the Williamsons chose to love me. Through music, college, graduate school, and changing career paths, there have never been bigger cheerleaders, Eric included. The year Eric and I were broken up was challenging for more reasons than I could count, but losing his family took the cake.

It was like going through two breakups at one time. That holiday season was rough. Not only was it my first without Eric in a decade, but it was also the first time I wasn't with Michelle. I had always dreaded Thanksgiving (remember the ham?) until joining in with the Williamsons.

Fun fact about me, I'm a very picky eater. I always have been and still struggle as an adult. It's a combination of sensory issues mixed with crazy things I've made up in my head. Either way, for some reason, Thanksgiving was the one day of the year my mom felt called to make me eat ham.

Being the stubborn human that I am and always have been, adolescent me spent most Thanksgivings sitting alone at the table for hours after everyone else was done, face-to-face with my stupid, single slice of ham. I don't recall ever actually eating it. I'll chalk it up to my pride and ego that in my memory I won that battle, but I do remember dreading Thanksgiving because of this, every single year.

Michelle and I had created our own traditions and she taught me a lot, including removing the giblets from a turkey and how to give it a salt bath. Remember the sensory issues I referenced? Let me just say, this was not a task I volunteered for again. If you don't happen to know what giblets are, spare yourself.

That year after the breakup, I felt like half of me was somewhere else. I would've given everything to rub down a thawing turkey with some salt. I remember a short text exchange on Thanksgiving Day where Michelle told me how much she loved me and missed me. I cried and cried, wishing I was with her. She always chose to love me, even in moments where Eric and I were still finding our way. She is the true embodiment of unconditional love.

I could write an entire encyclopedia about how this family changed me, shaped me, and believed in me. They set an extremely high standard for marriage, parenting, and family. They still do. The lesson, the life, and the love that Eric and I strive to embody every day is that unwavering loyalty to one another.

From our Grumpy Gramps and Grandma Nancy, now in Heaven, to Greg and Michelle, and Eric and me, the Williamson legacy isn't perfect, but very much worth living up to.

Eric and I chose to write our own vows at our wedding. During mine, I shared that Eric was the greatest gift I'd ever been given and the foundation that I stand on. That feeling remains true to this day. I was so excited to marry him and take his last name. Becoming a Williamson meant so much more to me and still does. I mean, Eric did make me wait long enough for it.

Unapologetic Truth #6: Family Worth Fighting For

Family is defined by the people who choose you, show up for you, believe in you, and unconditionally love you. Blood or not, they are the ones who accept you at your best, but also at your worst. They will support you, challenge you, and stand by you.

> If you don't have this at home and you haven't found this yet, don't lose hope. Find your family, find the people who feel like home, and find yourself.

Keep in mind that the right love and the right family are worth fighting for. Eric and I have fought for each other for almost two decades. Sometimes it's a walk in the park and at other times it's quite the opposite. Life will try to get in the way, and I promise it will throw you all sorts of curveballs. One of the greatest lessons the Williamsons have taught me is that not only do you get to choose your family, but you have to **keep** choosing them too, don't settle. You're worth it after all.

• • •

Chapter Seven

Sticks and Stones

• • •

Y'ALL KNOW THE SAYING, "Sticks and stones may break my bones, but words will never hurt me"? Well, I'm calling big ole bullshit on that one. Excuse my French, but it's true. For so long, I was conditioned to "toughen up," "ignore them," "let it go." My sister and I even had a song called, "Sticks and Stones" as part of our program against bullying. Words do hurt—they cut deep.

I can still recall the things I was called, bullied for, and made fun of. They flow in and out of my mind in moments of self-doubt even if said over a decade ago. There are a handful of moments I'd much rather have just been hit with a stick, stone, or both than be the recipient of the hateful comments that were said to me.

Many of us have been prey to the receiving end of bullying. But in all fairness, most of us have been the bearers of some not-so-nice moments too.

I shared with you briefly that there's a handful of people out there who I left worse than I found them. I won't stand before you (or write before you) and be too proud to admit that some of my worst moments reared their ugly head with me throwing daggers right back at the people throwing stones.

I won't play the blame game here. I own that in those moments I was completely wrong because two wrongs don't make a right. But what I will say is that when you were raised in a home that often felt like an episode of *Jerry Springer*, you quickly learned the damage you can do.

For those too young to know, *Jerry Springer* was the ultimate platform for raw, unfiltered drama before the days of social media. Guests aired their messiest personal problems on national TV, often ending in shouting matches and fistfights, with live audiences cheering like it was a wrestling match. It was chaotic, shocking, and impossible to turn away from.

As I've grown older, I like to think my skin has grown thicker and my spirit has grown calmer.

Unfortunately, even if you were bulletproof, when you wear your heart on your sleeve and start off loving people with all you've got, you're going to get burned. It's inevitable.

So I want to be honest with you, Eric would chime in here and say I still have a long way to go on this. I share that with you because he's right. I really do. And I want to hold myself accountable to that needed growth in hopes that if you have room to grow, it will inspire you to do the same.

I still get my feelings hurt more than I should and take things personally when they aren't meant to be, but progress over perfection. I have come a long way and still have room to grow.

I've hinted at the fact that I was criticized my whole life for my looks, my voice, my size, my choices, music—you name it. Oddly enough, I often still am. I think it comes with the territory of being "different."

While doing some deep-diving for the book, I happened to stumble upon an interview my sister and I did for an anti-bullying initiative (God-wink!). I was 17 at the time. I was asked by the interviewer why I felt I was bullied. What a question, right? I had to share my answer with you here:

> *I think now, in my generation, kids dealing with kids who are "different" are threatened or jealous and don't know how to deal with it in any other way but to bully. I know many of the times I was bullied was because I wasn't doing what everyone else was. And my message to kids who are different is this: Being different is ok!! It's kinda cool. Never change yourself for anyone!! God made you YOU for a reason and that reason is great.*

I must say, I still agree almost wholeheartedly with adolescent Cassy on this. I still believe that "different" makes most people uncomfortable, elicits the unknown, and can at times even feel threatening.

We don't know what we don't know, which can be scary.

So how do so many people respond to "different" (especially kids)? By tearing those individuals down or attempting to change what's different. Specifically, looking for a way to mask their own insecurities by belittling those around them who stand out.

So what made **me** so different?

For starters, my entire childhood was pretty much the "awkward phase." You saw the Annie photo. I was small with a big head and even bigger hair. There's a childhood photo of me that essentially looks like a little Cassy T. rex in a white turtleneck and grandma sweater.

Big head, small body, even tinier hands.

I was convinced from a young age by my mom that I was no natural beauty. I needed mascara, a tan, my hair done, and a full face of any makeup I could find to be pretty.

If I tried to leave the house as anything but, I could expect to hear about it. And even then, it was never a strong enough shield from her or my peers. There was always something to pick apart. To this day, you won't see me without mascara. I've shared with my inner circle that if there's a time that it does happen, call for help.

As funny as this may sound, I'm mostly serious. I won't allow myself to be "exposed" in that way.

As hard as I've worked on my mental health and self-talk, those scars run deep; most of my closest friends still haven't seen my face naked. I have come a LONG way, but I'm still a work in progress as I've shared with you. Aren't we all?

In middle school it was really my size and style. In high school it was anything physical you could think of. Even after all this time, growth, and success, I can still hear the words of the hateful voicemails I received almost weekly calling me a droopy-eyed-grandma-looking-hippie wannabe who shouldn't be alive.

Unfortunately, it didn't end with prank calls. Videos were made and posted online mocking me. Shirts were made to harass me. There was a photoshoot in my own front yard posted for all to see. My house was constantly a target.

I can't even count the number of weekends my poor dad started the day bright and early cleaning toilet paper out of our trees. This wasn't a fun tradition or prank that happened once or twice like some may think; this was a repeated effort to let me know what they thought of me. They had no mercy.

In some instances the bullying started simply. Simple meaning: I wore a cropped denim jacket to school and was told I was wearing clothes for "little people" and called hateful and very inappropriate names. Other times, the targeting was over a boy I liked or was dating. This included Eric. As our music career progressed, that became the next big target.

I didn't make it easy on myself by putting forth any effort to blend in, but I wouldn't go back and change that either.

A few bullies from my past have come to me and apologized. There are others who tortured me as long as they possibly could, only now to search me online or give me a "follow" on social media.

I believe that most of them were young and immature and have since grown up. But for others, I feel that they have a great deal of hate, jealousy, and spite in their hearts and likely continue to mock those around them, even as adults. Not everyone grows up—we all know the type.

But on top of the harassment I faced from my peers, the older I grew, the more the criticism also rolled in at home. My mom never shied away from reminding me when I became too heavy, too pale, or "let myself go." Not everyone could be a natural beauty like my sister, she would say to me.

Looking back, I wish I could see that 21-year-old me working full time, going to school full time, all while managing my own bills and expenses. That version of me was doing the best that she could with what she had. Sticks and stones.

For those of you who couldn't seem to escape the bullshit, whether at home or at school, you can probably relate to the heaviness of hearing the same song with just a different beat (I think I might've made that up) everywhere you went. It's exhausting.

★ When I get asked about my big "why" for this book, I want you to fold the page corner, do some underlining, pull out your highlighter, or make a note, whatever helps you remember this.

> We believe what we're told. We believe what we tell ourselves. In turn, when we're told enough, how ugly we are, how pointless our life is, or how much we're doing "it" (whatever that is) wrong, it gets heavy, and quick, especially for our younger generation.

I had low moments of self-harm and even darker ones where I questioned why I was here at all. And now, for every teen we lose to bullying, a piece of my heart breaks for them, their family, and for the life they could've had. If only they had just felt able to hang on.

I remember that pain, isolation, and self-doubt all too well. I remember the names, the faces, and the experiences I had with each of those girls, whether they do or not.

Now as a mom, I can't even fathom my girls being treated that way by their peers. I also can't imagine breathing anything but goodness about themselves into each of them. As a result, I'm overly sensitive about how I talk to myself in front of them.

I take great strides to remind my oldest how to think about herself, treat herself, talk to herself, and believe in herself. I'm not naive enough to think I can protect her from everything, but I do want them both to be confident, strong, and resilient so when life does try to rain on their parades, they don't let it wash them away.

The most bizarre part of all of this growing up was the piece of it that impacted me at home, the tug-of-war between tearing me down and building me up. Where my mom's words could and did rip me, my confidence, and my self-worth apart, so many times, she was also building me up if anyone else was tearing me down.

My parents believed in my sister and me; they supported our dreams and made sure we didn't "want" for anything. They both came from absolutely nothing and I think they felt like they were giving us what they didn't have. My question now is, at what cost?

But I'll tell ya, there was no question about it, when things got really bad at school, my mom couldn't get to the administrator's office fast enough. I just never understood why things were so different at home.

Unapologetic Truth #7: You are Not Alone

For some reason I always believed that when I survived school, graduated, "grew up," and moved out, all of this would be over. This being the emotional roller coaster of feeling like I had a target on my back for whatever mean moment life could throw my way. I was convinced it would be like making it out of the woods, just had to get to the other side. I couldn't have been the only one, could I?

Ignorance is bliss in so many ways when we're young and we don't know what we don't know. I wish that I could tell anyone younger reading this that with age, the drama, ugliness, and challenges dissolve, but I promised I'd be honest.

As we age, I think most of us can agree that life definitely changes, slightly shifts, and even evolves, but unfortunately, you need to expect that certain people will always be rooting against you. The best thing you can do is start practicing positive self-talk so early that its power outweighs any of that background noise.

But, if and when you have a completely human moment of self-doubt (because we all still do) and need reminding of how truly fantastic, special, and strong you are, lean into the tribe of people who will remind you of what you can't at that time remind yourself. The way you love yourself and the way your circle loves you **will** get you through.

If you don't have a circle yet, please know this: You are not alone. Did you get that? No matter how alone you may feel, you are not alone.

I have to share another quote from 17-year-old me in the interview I referenced earlier:

> *"You feel alone and think that no one will understand, but keeping it inside is the worst thing you can do. Talk to someone, whether it's your family, your teacher, your friend,* ***whoever****. It is so important to get it out. No one can carry that burden alone."*

For a long time I felt like I was alone, but I promise you your people are out there. Whether you're waiting for your Eric, your Williamsons, or your tribe, do not lose hope.

A dear friend of mine reminded me during a challenging season once, "You cannot control the behavior of others, but you can always choose how you respond to it."—Roy T. Bennett.

We're going to talk a lot more about finding your people and the fight for the light, but for now, remember it's hardly ever just sticks and stones and you **can** overcome those harsh words and moments.

• • •

Before We Get to Part Two…

You have to know that I didn't plan on going back this far into childhood and I definitely didn't anticipate sharing this much from my past with you. However, this section all but fell onto the pages so I'm taking that as my God-wink moment that it's a part of the story needing to be told.

> A God-wink moment is exactly what it sounds like. A little wink from Heaven! Some may call this a "sign from above," but I've always called them God-winks because I take them as moments where I feel like God is saying, "Yoohoo!! This is for you. Wink-wink, so pay close attention!" For the longest, I thought I was sitting with a Cassy-ism when really, God-winks are referenced in movies, books, and even have their own brand!!

Not to say reflecting back on these chapters of my life was easy; it definitely wasn't. In full transparency, I've blocked out so much of my childhood that I had to phone a friend a time or two to fact-check my own life. I wish I was kidding! I think that might be some sort of survival mechanism, both blocking out the bad and phoning a friend. Either way, I skimmed the surface just enough for you to hopefully understand.

It felt really important to me as I reflected on the book as a whole to give you the 20,000-foot view of my history growing up. My past has very much shaped the Cassy I was, the good and the bad. And it only made sense to share this with you first before leading you through the progression of being Unapologetically Me from then to now.

As important as it is to reflect on our own history, it's just as essential to highlight the importance of who we surround ourselves with. Who's your lifeline? Whether it's family, friends, or friends you call family. It doesn't only take a village to raise a child, it takes a village—**Period**.

I have been truly blessed by the people throughout my life saving me along the way. I clung to them and the hope they provided me. You'll hear those stories too. I'm here to say that being Unapologetic may start with yourself, but it definitely doesn't, can't, and shouldn't end there.

Part Two

Chapter Eight

The Fight for Light

• • •

BELIEVE IT OR NOT, I suffer from the crappiest, crippling anxiety that's made no better by ADHD. In my family, so much of this is genetic and very much untreated even now. Throw in depression, along with being a big empath, and here I am.

Did y'all know that being an empath is oftentimes a trauma response? This was just recently brought to my attention and that discovery hit me like a ton of bricks. Essentially, empaths have a heightened sensitivity to others' emotions which oftentimes was developed as a survival mechanism to maintain safety in their own relationships.

This response can stem from early experiences of trauma, leading one to prioritize others' emotions over their own as a form of self-protection and connection.

Simply put, I feel all the things, for all the people, in the biggest way and then stress about it all. To my fellow empaths out there: solidarity, friends, solidarity.

I will sob, agonize, and lose sleep over something as minute as a comment I made that might be taken the wrong way all the way to a news story happening states away. And that's just the tip of the iceberg.

I so badly wish I could take all the hurt, hate, and pain out of the world, and at times I'm delusional enough to think I can, one person at a time. I'm not ignorant to the fact that I've caused my own fair share of hurt and pain. Not claiming perfection here. But all in all, I'm a fixer who can't fix everything and that just frustrates the heck out of me.

You want to know what I long to fix the most? My family. You know who I ironically can't fix? My family. This is so humbling. If you're someone who comes from a lot of broken pieces, you aren't alone. There's a lot of us trying to find the puzzle we fit into without changing our shape (who we are).

As a kid, this feels like wanting to fit in. As I've grown older, I realized that fitting "in" wasn't how I'd describe it. What it came down to was finding where I could stand out and be accepted.

I was struggling with an issue at work and in a conversation with a dear friend, she said to me, "They're trying to put you in a box and you don't go in a box. You're not a person who can fit in a box."

As I reflected on that statement, I recognized that she's right. I haven't found a "box" I've fit in yet and I don't foresee that changing anytime soon. So I'd like to pose the argument that on the road to becoming Unapologetically You, rather than looking for where you fit "in," you should consider the opposite.

Where can you stand out and be accepted?

★ This will be your fight for light, your light. I challenge you to fight for what makes you the beautiful, Unapologetically You that you were meant to be. When you do, it will unleash the best experiences and relationships you could've ever dreamed of. I promise.

But in the midst of your fight for light, I warn you that it will not be all rainbows and sunshine. If it's anything like my experience, expect some turbulence.

My entire life has felt like fighting a torrential downpour in my favorite outfit, best pair of shoes, after I just got my hair done, without an umbrella, my hands full, oh and I lost the keys to my car.

Dramatic? Well, that would be one word you could use to describe my life. Insane? Another great word. Ridiculous, unthinkable, hard to imagine, too much, comical...y'all, I'm not kidding! Combine my already bad luck with a broken family and you've got the shitstorm of all shitstorms.

I've concluded that this is why I pour so much into other people. Because while I can't fix everything about my own situation, maybe I can help someone else. Maybe I can fix what they feel is broken. Maybe I can show them the grace the world hasn't yet shown them.

This is my fight for light; it's the fight for others to find their light.

Why? Because when you grow up in what feels like a constant "storm" with the sun just barely peeking out behind the clouds, you're going to fight like hell to find the rainbow on the other side, right?

My fight for light is made possible through you.

Like so many of us who love big, loud, and Unapologetically, you can count on me to be your biggest fan and most obnoxious cheerleader. I'm the friend you call when you need a pep talk, a corny GIF, and/or a hug (even if through the phone). I'm also the friend who will have no problem being your voice if you're having a hard time finding yours.

I will never let someone around me feel or be alone. And if you're reading this and you don't have that person in your life, please reach out to me. I mean it. Being a light, helping you through a storm, these are the greatest parts of my days.

★ Pouring value into others, encouraging them to see something they may not see in themselves, and lifting you up is my why. It's my attempt at making a difference, one person at a time.

One thing I'll admit to you is that I'm really good at preachin'. Practicing what I preach though? Well, that's another story and very much an uphill battle. Why? Because something I'm not as quick to share and something that may come as a surprise is that every day I'm what I'll call "Functioning and Fighting."

This is my made-up phrase that I use to describe myself, or anyone for that matter, who has to fight their own inner demons, trauma, and past regularly. Remember the anxiety, ADHD, and depression?

I'm not ashamed to share, even if I'm alone in this, that when you feel things as immensely as I do, you have to consciously fight your feelings too. My highs are very high, but my lows are unfortunately very low, and I can say with honesty that I don't really have an in between.

I don't love this, but I do live with it. I've found ways to navigate it. A big shift for me was learning to lean into the people around me instead of isolating myself. Even though I trust only a very select few people with my lows, I'm so fortunate to have a circle who will lift me on the days I can't lift myself. I hope and pray you have this too.

Thankfully, at this point in my life, on most days and in most situations, I **choose** the light. I **choose** to be happy, **find** the happy, and most importantly **share** the happy.

Unapologetic Truth #8: Choose the Light

I don't use the word "choose" lightly. For me it is a choice. And for most of us, we have to **choose** our path. Every day. Happiness is a choice. Positivity is a choice. Love is a choice.

Fighting for the light is the **hard** fight. I promise you on some days it'll be handed to you like a perfectly frosted cake with sprinkles on top, but on other days it'll feel almost impossible. Despite what the day has dealt you, you have to fight for the light. Lean into your faith here because there will always be a light, if only a glimmer, to look for.

Whether it's a person in your life, a place you're drawn to, or an outlet…establish a process that works for you to find the light. Be open to the people around you who love you and lean on them when you need to. You're not fighting this battle alone, my friend. We're all out here doing just the best we can.

A friend shared a fantastic message going around by Kennedy Simone that depicts how darkness can't and won't take from darkness. I'll paraphrase her sentiment: darkness can only take from the light. So when it feels like you're being attacked from every angle, it's because you are light. Keep choosing the light, it's worth it. You are worth it.

DISCLAIMER: Please keep in mind that my situation is just that, my situation. My mental health is only that, mine. No one knows you better than you know yourself. Don't keep yourself from seeking the help you feel that you need or reaching out for a lifeline. No one should have to fight for their light alone.

• • •

Chapter Nine

No, You Tone It Down

• • •

I COULD USE THIS CHAPTER as my burn book to list the people, places, and situations that either nicely or not so nicely pushed me to change who I was, hence the phrase, "tone it down." I've got a long mental list of teachers, instructors, friends, managers, and even people I looked up to who in some form wanted me to compromise my "me."

But I won't do that here. What good does that do now?

Instead, I want to reflect on why. How frequently are the fantastic, beautiful, and talented individuals around us being asked to compromise who they are for another's comfort? Comfort being what's familiar, what's habitual, and what's expected.

This phenomenon doesn't discriminate either; it's rampant. Who do we see as the most consistent focus? From my observations, it's those who go against the grain. Whether it's personally, professionally, or both, they are consistently at the receiving end of a "tone it down" request.

Why? Familiarity breeds comfort. Familiarity fits what's already in place. Familiarity is safe. I'm not saying that what's familiar is always wrong. I'm very familiar with the beach and it will never be "wrong" to love it and wish I was there more often. But how do we respond to consistent backlash when we're leaning into being our most Unapologetic Self?

Personally, I've been asked to "tone it down" more times than I can count. It's been going on for well over a decade and yet it still hurts like it was the first time all over again. It's like being dumped. It may keep happening, but it doesn't mean you enjoy the experience.

I shared that when I was 14, I was asked to stop singing in my "Cassy voice" by my high school choir teacher. This is the first time I remember distinctly feeling pushed to change "me" to get to a successful outcome. If I wanted the solo, more opportunities to showcase my voice, or even a better spot in the school musical, I had to stop being (or singing) the "Cassy Way."

But do you know what? I didn't listen, partially because I had no idea how to stop singing in my "Cassy voice" and partially out of pure stubbornness. Either way, two short years later my sister and I were sponsored by the National Guard on a national level to speak and sing to military leaders, families, and youth.

So you know what I say to that and what I hope you do too? "No, you tone it down."

Fast forward to my professional career and as recently as this past year, I was told by an industry leader that they weren't sure how I'd be received by high-level executives. They expressed concerns that my success would be inhibited because my energy level and personality would likely keep me from being taken seriously in a corporate setting. Two words: gut punch. After all this time, here it was again, "tone it down."

Whether it was my voice, my appearance, my personality, or my energy level—pick a trait and I've been asked to change, modify, or omit it from the environment I found myself in.

Do not take this as your get-of-jail-free card for any and all behaviors. Constructive criticism is just that. We should always be receptive to opportunities for growth and ways to challenge ourselves. It's never okay to continuously act like a jerk and claim that you're being Unapologetic. Okay, back to our regularly scheduled programming.

So how do we handle this?

With grace, poise, and just a little bit of sass. But even then, after all this time, I still have moments that rock the boat and bring me to tears. Despite how far I've come, I'm a person (just like you) and I'll remind you that it is 1000% okay to feel your feelings, especially when asked to give up your "you." I definitely do.

I'll let you in on a not-so-little secret: I'm an easy crier. I have never felt a movie scene more than Jude Law in *The Holiday* spoken in my best British accent… "I cry all the time…I'm a major weeper." That's just me and I'm okay with that.

The most detrimental moments I've found myself in, and I caution you on this, are those when I'm let down by a person or place that I was sure would be "different," specifically, when a person or place turns out to be something I didn't think they would be.

Have you been there too? Have you ever gambled on someone, gone all in, and then ended up feeling like you've been catfished?

What about work? Ever made a transition to an organization that on the outside looked like the next best thing, but winds up having the same depth as the chocolate shell on a peanut M&M?

It absolutely sucks. No reason to sugarcoat it, even if I did my best with a candy reference.

Being misled all to just be put right back in this same situation is upsetting, especially if you also feel taken by surprise. Process that as you need to, but I'd challenge you here. It is imperative that you don't lose yourself to emotion when faced with these challenges.

Resist the urge to:

1. Set up camp in that space and throw an extended pity party
2. Even slightly consider the change they are asking of you
3. Let them dull your shine.

So what's the solution?

Do you happen to have a green thumb? I know nothing about plants and can barely keep two summer ferns alive, but I do know when it comes to plants flourishing, we (people) actually have a lot in common.

I want you to take a moment to reflect on a time you found yourself in a toxic environment, relationship, or even team or company culture.

- Were you your best self?
- Did you experience growth?
- Were you happy?

If the answer to any or all of these questions was "No," we have to ask "Why?"

> To grow and thrive, we have to be extremely selective in the environments we choose and allow ourselves to be in. Why? Because when kept in the wrong space, planted in the wrong pot, or put in a bad habitat, plants can't survive. The same thing is true for us. Who we surround ourselves with and where we place ourselves will dictate how we grow and evolve.

This is not a foolproof system. I so badly wish I had it figured out for you. It's essentially impossible for us to avoid this entirely, but what I want you to take away is something I wish I would've made peace with and accepted a lot earlier in life.

The moment, and I mean **moment**, that a person or place asks you to compromise something about yourself that you know to be good, take it as your God-wink to make your exit.

Not walk off the job that day and fail to pay your bills because you read this book and I said "leave." BUT—recognize that when this happens, it is your big, bright, red flag screaming that either the person or space can no longer serve you, develop you, or support you.

You not only deserve those things, but require them on this journey to being Unapologetically You.

Unapologetic Truth #9: Exit to Elevate

For as long as I can remember, I've had no problem walking away from people, places, or situations that don't allow me to be Unapologetically Myself. Not to say that it's a flawless system. Was I strong in every situation? No. Did it always happen immediately? I wish. Did I stand up for myself or others loudly or boldly every time I could've? Regretfully not.

Why does this matter? Because setting boundaries, walking away from spaces that don't serve you, standing up for yourself, having a voice, or using your voice for others—none of this elicits or requires perfection. We can't and won't be that.

The risk of going into this expecting to get it right every time will only impair our progress. Specifically, we're more likely to shy away from moments and circumstances we should actually lean into.

As I've grown more consistent with this, I've been pleasantly surprised to discover that by forfeiting time in the wrong space, you end up finding the people, places, and situations that ARE worth fighting for. Specifically, ones that allow you to be uniquely you, Unapologetically You. I can assure you this doesn't happen overnight, as these kinds of people aren't everywhere.

But a piece of advice: Once you've found them, give them everything you've got. Don't hold back even if you've been burned in the past. Don't doubt yourself. Don't even question what could go wrong. Throw yourself into these opportunities and I assure you some of your greatest moments of learning, growth, and love will transcend.

• • •

Chapter Ten

The Angels Among Us

• • •

HAVE YOU HEARD the song "Angels Among Us" by Alabama? In short, the song is all about the angels around us. The people who quietly guide us and teach us to live, give, and lead with love.

> If you happen to be a sap like I am and also like extremely corny '90s anything, after this chapter, grab a box of tissues, and go watch the music video from 1994.

The idea for this song and also what I strive to highlight in this chapter is the belief that in our life, there are Angels Among Us, placed in our life to teach us, guide us, and show us love in some of our more challenging moments.

It's amazing how even in the darkest of times, God will show us light and life through the people around us, specifically the Angels Among Us. But you have to be open to receiving them too.

Although I've made a crappy case for school, I won't deny that some of the most impactful people in my life came from a classroom or somewhere close to it.

For those of you in education, you are a true gift to the children and families around you. You may never know what happens outside of your classroom walls, but if you need a reminder today of your impact, here it is. Your gifts have a larger purpose, and you may never know the influence you have on a child's life, but believe in the power of what you do.

These individuals modeled exactly what I needed to grow into my Unapologetic Self, preemptively changing the course of my life.

My hope for this chapter is that I can pass along their teachings as lessons. I also hope it encourages you to not only look for, but reflect on the impact of the angels around you because I'm confident they are there.

So much so that I hope you already have an angel or two of your own in mind.

Angel One:

Doris was the secretary at my elementary school, a warm-hearted woman I called my adopted grandma. Despite having her own kids and grandkids, she chose to show up as family for so many of us who weren't her own. That was her gift.

During pivotal moments in my life, Doris was a constant. She spent birthdays, holidays, and many weekends with us. She was also there in more challenging moments.

Doris was the one who discovered I was struggling with self-harm in high school. And just like every moment leading up to this one, she met me with compassion, love, grace, and support. She went above and beyond to make sure it didn't continue, that I knew my value and understood my worth; for that I am indebted to her forever.

Her Lesson: Doris taught me (and all of those around her) that **there's no cap on love.** There's no limit on how much you can care for people. She took in so many "kids" and treated everyone like family. She was Unapologetic in how she showed up for all of those around her and her life was a testimony to how much one heart can love.

Angel Two:

Sister Clara was the spunkiest, sassiest "sister" I had and probably will ever meet. I had the great fortune of sitting with her at the Motherhouse every week and oh, how we would laugh. She would take any crappy day and help me find my light. She was the kind of person who could find joy in anything, only because she chose to.

Sister Clara's gift was that she truly loved like Jesus, openly and without judgment. She never tried to change who you were, but only encouraged you to love and live by His example.

Her Lesson: Sister Clara will always serve as my reminder that **we can show up just as we are, wherever we are, and still serve our purpose**. You don't have to compromise your quirky, tone down what's "loud" about you, or hide your weird to fulfill your calling.

Sister Clara dedicated her entire life to religious vows of poverty, chastity, and obedience all the while being spunky, loud, and totally against the grain.

This was not your typical "sister." But her "why" was never compromised by her "how" and I loved that so much about her. We can all strive to embody that same example.

Angel Three:

Sister Peggy was my theology teacher freshman year, and she was the first lifeline I was given at my new school, well before Eric.

Her kindness and patience were truly saint-like and she only lost me with her strategy at assigning partners for the year. I have still not forgotten about when she chose to pair me up with the grumpiest, quietest, most challenging classmate we had.

I stayed after class the day Sister Peggy made the pairing announcement, begging her to spare me the awkwardness and the challenges this partnership would cause. I distinctly remember saying, overdramatically, "Sister Peggy, I thought you liked me?! Why would you pair me with him for an entire year?!" and her response will live with me forever.

She said, "Because, Cassy, I know you'll be nice to him. I can count on you to treat him the way he deserves to be treated," Mic Drop. And so that's exactly what I was to him, for the entire year. She believed I would, so I did.

Through this experience, she taught me one of the most valuable life lessons.

Her Lesson: Those who often need our kindness, grace, and compassion the most are typically the people who are least likely to show it.

And by the end of the year, he and I had bonded. Were we best friends? No. But he knew that he had a friend in me and I had a friend in him. We'd look out for one another, talk to each other, and root for the other's success.

Angel Four:

Mr. Lavin had been teaching for over 40 years when I entered his classroom my junior year, which made him older, wiser, and one-of-a-kind. He was so wonderfully quirky and Unapologetically Himself. He was both a fantastic human AND teacher.

Mr. Lavin was so dedicated and gave his entire life to education. He also believed (he's still working on it) that he could solve the assassination of JFK.

If that didn't bring a smile to your face, read it again. How many teachers did you have working to crack the case?

In addition to history, Mr. Lavin taught me how to be bold, brave, and believe that anything was possible.

We became pen pals after high school. Being the sap that I am, I've saved and cherished them all, but my most favorite note (and lesson) was one that he wrote me during a lecture on 12/10/2008.

His Lesson: **"Miss Gaddis—Whatever you become, strive to be as good as you can. Take pride in what you do. In that there is great wealth."**

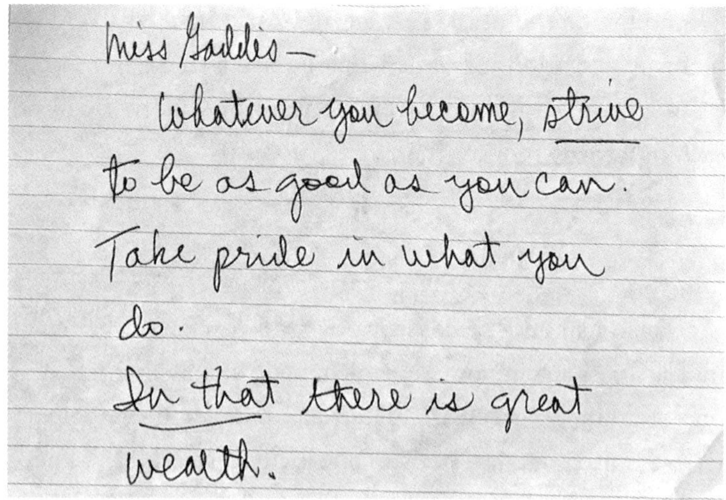

Miss Gaddis—
Whatever you become, strive to be as good as you can.
Take pride in what you do.
In that there is great wealth.

Angel Five:

I was gifted with Dr. Clark while obtaining my bachelor's degree. I'm attracted to the wonderfully spunky, and Dr. Clark was no exception.

Dr. Clark had been teaching at MTSU for over 20 years and is one of the most intelligent women I have ever known. In addition to being absolutely brilliant, she was slightly unorganized and a bit of a hoarder.

I can't tell you the **hours** I spent sitting between book towers talking about school, life, and everything in between. Her smile lights up an entire room. Her love, passion, and heart for not only the field, but also her students were her superpower.

As someone who was a rising star during segregation, discrimination, and moments of unimaginable hate, she taught me that the only way to meet people is with love—no matter how they choose to treat you.

Her Lesson: Dr. Clark embodies that when it comes to your dreams, your passions, and your goals—there is truly nothing that can hold you back. **You are unstoppable when you believe in yourself.** Even when it feels like the entire world is against you (and sometimes it is), there is nothing that can hold you back from your own success if you're unwilling to give up.

Angel Six:

Last in my educational journey, a cherished mentor and friend, Beth, my final graduate supervisor and largely the very reason I had my first job opportunity before even graduating.

In addition to driving me to be an exceptional clinician, thinking outside of the box, and remaining flexible throughout the process, Beth was also a large contributor in helping me become and embrace my very best self.

Her patience, effectiveness, empathy, and aptitude for evaluating a caseload filled with extremely complex kids made her nothing short of a blessing. She carried those same traits into most all of her relationships.

Her Lesson: **Ensure that everyone you interact with feels loved, seen, heard, and valued.**

Unapologetic Truth #10:
The Power of Presence

Y'all want to know what every single one of these humans had in common?

Before I answer—it wasn't fame, fortune, or power. It wasn't the highest position of leadership, millions of followers, the biggest platform, or unlimited resources.

What each of them had in common was an unwavering dedication to improving the lives of their students. They were fully invested in bettering the lives of those around them. They cared deeply and genuinely about the people they served.

I think that we at times convince ourselves that we need all of these external things to make a significant impact, but we're largely mistaken.

Their lessons prove the concept that we all have the power to Make a Difference—from whatever position we find ourselves in.

Their impact was so great that I wrote a song about it.

The lyrics have shaped who I am, how I live, and what I strive to be. They're framed behind my desk to remind me daily that we all have the ability to change someone's life exactly as we are, no matter where we are.

Wondering how you find your own Angels?

Start by asking the questions below…

1. Who in your life has made a significant impact?
2. What lesson do you feel they taught you?

3. Have you longed to emulate that same characteristic or lesson in your own life?

Once you've identified a few of your own Angels, I'd challenge you to then reflect on these questions…

1. Do they know their impact on your life?
2. What are you doing today to make the same positive impact?
3. How do you pay it forward?
4. Better yet, where do you have an immediate opportunity?

Do not skip over this.

If you're feeling uncomfortable, good. Get comfy with being uncomfy; it means that growth is happening.

If you're on the road to being Unapologetically You, I'm confident that there have been people along the way who have encouraged you to do so.

I'm going to challenge you now to pay that forward. I would not be the person I am today without the people I mentioned above…and these were just some of the main characters of my story. Who are yours?

• • •

Chapter Eleven

Love 'em Down

• • •

FULL DISCLOSURE, Eric told me I **really** shouldn't use this phrase to name this chapter or describe my concept (now or ever), but just like many other times, I hear him, appreciate his insight, but am going with it anyways because if this was meant for you, you'll get it. If it wasn't, that's just fine too. I'm very aware it's not for everyone.

Y'all know how we talk about wearing people down? Or maybe even wearing them out? I can be exhausting to some. I know this about myself. I have a **lot** of energy and I bring it to the table every day.

If you haven't eaten your Wheaties, people like me should come with a warning label. And as I've shared, people like me aren't for everyone (those aren't our people). **But** one of my greatest joys in life is "loving people down" especially for *on-the-fencers*.

Wondering what it means to be an *on-the-fencer?* You should, because this is a concept I created for my favorite people to love on. An on-the-fencer is a fantastic human who finds themself a bit more "in the middle" than where you'd find someone like me.

Now, they aren't hanging out in a completely different yard like a Scrooge, but no one is calling them Buddy the Elf as their first impression either.

When I meet an *on-the-fencer,* whether personally or professionally, I get **so** excited (and I hope you do too). Why? Because these are the people who need us the most!

Their sparkle, spunk, light, quirkiness, or whatever word you want to use to describe it **is** already inside of them; it's a part of who they were meant to be. But it needs a bit of gentle nudge or wake-up call from someone like us! Bring that turtle right out of its shell, y'all.

A true *on-the-fencer* isn't going to open up easily. They're not giving it up for free. If anything, they're going to make you work for it. But oh my goodness, when you get there… when that part of them comes to life…when you love 'em down…just picture that scene from *The Grinch* where his heart grows three sizes after being loved on by Cindy-Lou Who. It feels **that** good.

But have you seen *The Grinch*? If you haven't, let me fill you in. Cindy-Lou could be described with one word: intentional (maybe persistent too). And just like her, when it comes to our sweet on-the-fencers, the intentionality is left to us.

I want you to take a moment to think about your daily routine. How many choices a day do you think you make? According to the 2023 *Harvard Business Review* article "A Simple Way to Make Better Decisions" by Amanda Reilly, we make an average of 33,000 to 35,000 choices a day. Holy. Cow.

Most days, my routine begins with choosing my little heart out before the sun is even up. What about you? I have to choose what my daughter will wear, what I'll wear, what we'll eat, what we'll drink, where we'll go, and so on.

Luckily, so many of the choices we make are automatic and thus require less effort. I'm talking about choices like taking a shower, brushing your teeth, and putting on deodorant. Please do that, choose that. ☺

But something I think we often fail to consider is our level of intentionality with the choices we make about the "world" around us. Even more so, how do we choose to respond to the people we encounter? Strangers included.

I believe that your perspective on these choices will dictate the spirit, vibe, and even outcome of your day.

Do you look at these moments as gifts? Opportunities? A curse?

If you haven't considered it, please do that with me now.

We get to choose how we greet the person walking in the door ahead of us. We decide how we respond to the person riding our you-know-what in traffic. We also get to choose how we respond to whatever chaos our kids decide to dabble in, all before we even walk out the door.

Before we get too far along, if you struggle with how you respond to others, consider this an opportunity for growth. A great first step. You may even want to look up *The Negativity Fast.* It will provide you with a very interesting perspective on how to shape your own responses when the world around you seems to be absolutely losing its marbles (because let's face it, that is not changing). If you're a leader reading this, it's also a fantastic challenge to try with your team.

So this is the moment of truth. This is where the choice chimes in.

Most look at an *on-the-fencer* as a pain in the ass, not an opportunity. Most stand in front of this person thinking something like, "What's their problem?", "Who do they think they are?", "What side of the bed did they wake up on today?" (These are the PG versions, you're welcome.)

We've all been there. We've all been faced with situations that rock the boat, inconvenience our plan, or challenge our sanity. Doesn't the universe know you're just trying to have a good day over here?

The more we have to interact with these people, on whatever level, the more we may start feeling like "Anger" from *Inside Out*. Trust me, I still have days where I need to internally slap my sassy self and remember the mission: Love. Them. Down.

Time for some self-reflection…ever been having the crappiest day and a random stranger did something that instantly restored your faith in humanity? (God-winks).

Take a minute to think about that moment specifically and ask yourself these questions.

1. What was going wrong with my day?
2. Where was I?
3. What was I feeling?
4. Who intercepted the moment?
5. How did that act of kindness shift my perspective?

Do you have this moment in your mind?

DO NOT skip ahead if you don't.

Don't even think about it.

If for some reason you cannot come up with a single moment to guide you through this exercise, I'll give you mine to borrow. However, don't let this chapter pass you by without looking for a moment like this in your own life. Fold the page, highlight it, flag it...Deal?

During my training on the customer experience, I highlight my sweet friend Chad. Let me introduce you.

Ever been personally victimized by a foreign object in your tire?

I was headed out of town for a work trip where I'd be driving through the Chattahoochee-Oconee National Forest where I'd already been warned that although the views were fantastic, the route was very much off the grid.

My car was packed, but as I headed out, I was greeted by a flat tire. I knew that I needed to get to my closest option for help which happened to be Tire Discounters. I pulled into the lot with a line out the door when out walked a man with glasses, a baseball cap, grease up to his elbows, and an accent so thick I just imagined Matthew McConaughey in Los Angeles.

As he was removing the tire from my car for inspection, I quickly learned that this man's name was Chad. He'd been working on cars for most of his life, had a 5-year-old son, and was close to his family.

After returning with my tire, Chad gave me that look. He said, "Ma'am, there's a razor blade in your tire and I've never seen one jammed in there like that before." Lucky. Me.

I was on the road to nowhere but **late** as Chad explained that company policy doesn't allow them to patch tires, but they could sell me a new one. Chad was aware of my dilemma and after a bit of back-and-forth agreed to attempt to patch my tire so I could get on the road, but he provided no guarantees.

When Chad came back, he had my tire in hand and shared that he was able to patch the tire and soon I'd be on my way. As he was putting the tire back on my car, I expressed my nerves about traveling alone, in the mountains, with no cell service… Remember the Chattahoochee?

With the deepest sincerity, he looked me in the eye and said, "Ma'am, I wouldn't put you in this vehicle if I also wouldn't put my mama in it. And I would."

That's all I needed to hear, I was ready to go.

But guess what? Chad's kindness didn't stop there. He proceeded to ask me if I had a spare tire, just in case. I shared that I had no idea and even if I did, I wouldn't know the first thing about changing a tire.

With the line still out the door, appointments on the books, and a clearly demanding day ahead, Chad said, "Let's check it out." And it was there in the middle of the Tire Discounters parking lot that Chad taught me how to change a tire.

I'd like you to reflect for just a moment on how empowered I felt. My morning went from complete disaster to completely saved. I was leaping through the parking lot, ready to tackle whatever was thrown my way, and called everybody and their brother to tell them about Chad. What an experience!

Now, if this random moment of kindness could so strongly impact my day, don't we have the same power?

When you're met with reluctancy or reservations, especially when being Unapologetic, I want you to look at this as an opportunity or maybe even a *challenge* if you're competitive like me.

I want you to meet these individuals with all the kindness, love, energy, and freakin' sparkle you've got. Channel your inner Cassy or your inner Chad. Keep in mind that both ways work!

Take them by surprise with consistency, patience, and love and watch them transform. Whether it's someone you work with, someone you're having a harder time building a relationship with, or maybe even someone in your own circle or family. Take a moment to go out of your way to love 'em down.

A true *on-the-fencer* will blow you away and leave you feeling fulfilled (and even victorious). They will transform before you. Some transformations may be grand, but others may be more slight. The important thing to remember is that your love, your kindness, your sincerity, and your consistency allowed them to show you a part of them they don't meet others with openly.

They go from being *on-the-fence* to off and over it. They trust you, they lean into you, and they will look to you during moments where maybe they weren't able to before with the other people around them.

Unapologetic Truth #11: Boldly Share Kindness

You want to talk about an absolute gift? I can't think of anything better than watching someone who met you with reservations and reluctance recognize that you're someone they can trust. Someone who, even if just in that moment, can restore their faith in humanity.

This is like running down the stairs at seven years old on Christmas Day. It's magic.

Want to know the craziest, coolest part of leaning into this? You will change lives doing this while also changing your own.

Maybe it's a small moment, but maybe it's much bigger. Some of my most beloved, inner circle and closest friends started off as *on-the-fencers.* I'm so grateful for the time I took to love 'em down. I know they'd tell you they're grateful too. They're so stinkin' worth it.

So who are the *on-the-fencers* in your life that you need to lean into? Who do you feel a tug to spend a little bit more time on? I'd encourage you to start with those people first and build. Take it in baby steps, one person at a time. And then, when you're feeling confident and ready, go out there and shine your light with the strangers around you. Love 'em down. Be a Chad.

Warning: Not everyone is an *on-the-fencer.* That's right, I said it and be warned. Not every person wants to receive kindness, grace, and love. I can tell you from firsthand experience. So let me tee you up for these moments, since no one did for me.

There will be individuals who will retreat even further into their "shells" in response to your efforts. They will snuff and turn their noses up at your attempts to break through. Some people are not looking for joy, and as sad as that is, you've got to learn to be okay with this too.

Now as someone who takes things very personally, I'm preaching to the choir on this one. But you cannot let an instance like this keep you from trying again and then trying some more. The victories far outweigh the losses here. Trust me on this one. Go out there and keep trying to love 'em down because the world needs us to.

• • •

Chapter Twelve

Find Your Tribe

• • •

IN WEEDING THROUGH (who knew I'd come up with so many plant references) people and places, I've gone through 'em, y'all. The good, the bad, and the ugly. In that process, I've also found the **really** freaking fantastic, the people whom I'm fortunate enough to call my tribe.

This space has no competition, jealousy, or spite. These beautiful individuals embrace me as I am, love me through it all, hold me up when I can't seem to stand, encourage me, and support me through every one of life's highs and lows. I can be whoever I need to be in front of them.

But much like Rome, this tribe wasn't built in a day. Unlike a lot of people, I had to wait a **long** time, arguably too damn long, for this tribe. I never had "the" childhood bestie who I met in kindergarten and then stood by my side on my wedding day. I wish I did, but I think moving schools every two seconds while also having a family straight out of a TV drama made that a bit challenging. Being a total weirdo didn't help me either.

Along the way, I've had my fair share of friends, most of whom were friends who served me in the stage of life I was in. The friends I made at work, friends I had classes with, friends I ran with in college. Few and far between are anything more than a friend on social media. Most of these friendships didn't last long, grow, or evolve much past the phase of life we found ourselves in.

Growing apart, falling out of touch, or losing some of these people completely was always a challenge for me.

For the longest time I struggled with the "why" until I stumbled upon this quote:

"There is a purpose for everyone you meet. Some people will test you, some will use you, some will bring out the best in you, but everyone will teach you something about yourself." —Anonymous

---

This message resonated with me then and still rings true in my journey to finding my tribe. Throughout every friendship, I've learned more about myself, about relationships, and about who I want to be. I've been challenged by different personalities, beliefs, and values. I've been hurt by insincerity and insecurity.

I recognize the perfect friend doesn't exist and I won't claim to be one either. Plenty of people along the way got a very imperfect, broken, working version of me. But for every one of them, I'm grateful because they taught me something that allowed me to grow.

Although many of these relationships didn't turn out the way I hoped or envisioned for one reason or another, I remind myself of the sentiment above. And I hope in sharing this, you'll consider the same in your own relationships.

We can't be scared of the ending before something has even begun. Just like a really bad breakup. We've all lost friends. And I'd argue, in many instances, these losses hurt worse than a breakup. But we can't be scared of failed relationships without sacrificing the opportunity to find the really good ones in the process of searching.

So how do you find your tribe? What does it take to find your people? Honestly, there's no right or wrong answer here. I don't believe in a secret friend formula that pops out the "right friend" every time. I know I've found my people in some of the craziest, most unexpected spaces and places.

What I can say is that I remain open to anyone and everyone and I'd encourage you to do the same. You just never know who God is trying to put in your life at that moment. And ultimately, I believe that He has a bigger plan for each and every person that comes in and out of our lives if we open ourselves up to it.

But along this journey, I've learned a hard truth that I want to share with you, hoping it will guide and protect you on your way to finding your own tribe.

Similar to how I do a lot of things, I love people quickly, loudly, proudly and do so without many limits. I have no shame in telling you just how much I love you. This has served me well in some friendships, but has absolutely burned me in others. What I've found consistently is that love and trust should not always be given out concurrently.

For the longest time, I gave both love and trust up for grabs, way too soon. I was willing to love on someone AND let my guard down without hesitation. I felt like by giving someone both, I opened myself up to the kind of friend I always wanted and wished I had.

But with this strategy comes great heartache.

Why? Because unfortunately, the wrong people will take your transparency, vulnerability, honesty, and love and use it for anything but good. Maybe at first it's more slight, but as time goes on, with the wrong people, you are only opening yourself up to a world of hurt.

I've experienced this the hard way, repeatedly, after way too many failed attempts. Fool me once, shame on you, fool me twice, shame on me—not sure what happens after fooling me three, four, or five times, but hear me when I say I've let this system play out (and fail) with one too many people. So although you can love big, loud, and proud, and I hope you do, I encourage you to protect yourself by being slower to trust.

Unapologetic Truth #12: Connection Over Convenience

As you navigate relationships in your own life, share what you feel called to share. But I caution you to recognize that reservations about who you let come into your circle, your life, and your family's life is a healthy boundary. It's similar to the saying, "When you know, you know." Trust your instincts, maintain your value, don't compromise, and wait for your *tribe*. These humans are worth waiting for, I promise.

Don't be scared of giving people a chance. We will never know if we don't try, right? **But don't be confined to convenience.**

Restricting yourself with people just like you, people who are physically close to you, or relationships that have just gotten comfortable will hold you back from your bigger purpose.

There's something to be said about the discussion around how we "become" or are the "average" of the five people we surround ourselves with the most. I don't know about you, but if I'm the average of those five people, I want them to be off the charts. If they are, I have no other choice but to be too.

How do the people around you elevate you?

Seek out the people who love you just as you are, encourage you to be your best self, and inspire you to grow into exactly who you were meant to be. And be that for them too. Friendship is a two-way street. It's give and take. It takes effort, work, and intentionality just like any good relationship. When you're building your tribe, don't settle for anything less than people who fill your cup. Be wary toward those who consistently take from it.

Once you've found them, hold on with all you've got. They're the diamonds in the rough. They're the Angels Among Us. Pour into them as they pour into you. Don't settle for anything less.

(And for my tribe reading this, I love you more than words could ever say. I couldn't and wouldn't want to do life without you. I'm so blessed and thankful for each of you. This chapter is for you.)

• • •

Chapter Thirteen

Deep-End Friends

• • •

THIS LEADS ME RIGHT INTO one of my favorite spots, the *deep end...* see what I did there?

You know when you go to the pool, you normally have two choices? Or you're one of two kinds of people?

Person number one walks over to the stairs, eases their way into the shallow end, and slowly acclimates themself to the water.

Person number two walks right over to the edge of the deep end and jumps in without hesitation. You know who you are. We love you for it.

Although y'all must know I'm not about to do a cannonball at the pool for more than one reason, when it comes to friendships, I'm all about the deep end. I call these the really good ones, my *deep-end friends.*

Before we jump in (yes, it's another pool pun!), let me distinguish your inner circle from a deep-end friend.

Your inner circle would be the friends you've taken the journey with. You've navigated your way through the shallow end toward the deepest part of the pool. They're a part of your tribe and you share a history. You've been through both joys and hardships and remained close.

Your inner circle knows most of what there is to know about you. You're also likely integrated in their day-to-day life and fully invested in their world, which could be their family, career, pets, hobbies, etc. These are the friends that you could be in any part of the "pool" with, thanks to your history and bond. These friendships are rare and for many of us, having a few would be considered lucky.

But what about the people you've met along the way either professionally or personally and instantly clicked with? I said it earlier and I believe it: "When you know you know." This is just that. You'll have no history, make little effort, yet feel an immediate connection.

You can dive into thoughtful conversations with meaningful exchanges about your goals and aspirations, and these individuals, they just get it. The best part is that your deep-end friend will not only get it, but they'll support your efforts in getting you where you want to go.

These are the high achievers and big dreamers. You may not have the same history as other friends or speak on a regular basis, but when you connect, it's like picking up where you left off with conversations that provide substantial impact.

Now, with my deep-end friends, I really don't know the intimate details of their life. I couldn't tell you their dog's name, what high school they went to, what exactly their spouse does for work, or the name of their hometown. But I do know that when I need guidance, vision, accountability, or inspiration, these are the friends I call and vice versa.

Our deep-end friends are exactly as they sound. They're the friends we jumped right in and got deep with. They're the ones we speak to on a higher level with raw vulnerability so that we can challenge and elevate one another.

Deep-end friends act as mentors, advisors, and confidants with no further explanation needed. It can be weeks without a discussion, but when you're in need, your deep-end friends are ready and willing to dive in, strategize, and see you through it.

Do you know who these individuals are in your life?

This is not a question to ignore because these friends are going to be instrumental in your growth, success, and the journey to being Unapologetic.

Here's a few questions to ask when considering your deep-end friends…

1. When I'm struggling with a challenging conflict, who do I call for direction?
2. If I have a big decision to make, with an unclear choice, who typically provides me the most level-headed and/or impactful advice?
3. Who provides me insight fueled by integrity and without bias?
4. Who can I dream big with?
5. Who believes in me even when I don't see it in myself?

I consider and treat these humans to be real-life treasures. I hold them close, refuse to take them for granted, and know that they're true rarities. I recognize that deep-end friends require give-and-take, and this is an extremely important part of sustaining these relationships.

I joke that these friendships are like a tennis match serving back-and-forth. As much as these friends pour into you, you have to be willing (and able) to pour into them. Deep-end friendships don't feel like work, but they also require intentionality, love, and a great deal of respect.

When evaluating the relationships in your own life, please keep in mind that your tribe, inner circle, and deep-end friends are NOT drama facilitators in your life. The intention of anyone in your circle is to make your life brighter and lighter, NOT harder.

Unapologetic Truth #13: Impact Over Effort

The best thing about deep-end friends is that these are some of the most effortless friendships in your life.

High-maintenance individuals cannot serve you as deep-end friends. You can't be high-maintenance in the deep end; there's one word for that and it's drowning. The wrong "friends" will make you feel like you're drowning too.

These friendships are not bound by any sort of limitations so don't overthink it. What you do, where you live, how old you are, or where you come from, none of it matters with these beautiful humans.

You'll feel an overwhelming sense of peace when you find your deep-end friends. You know you're in the presence of "your people." So once you've found them, hold on to them with everything you've got. Goodness attracts more goodness, and this part of your tribe will change your world.

Don't be afraid to jump in!

* * *

Chapter Fourteen

God-Winks

• • •

Y'ALL, I DIDN'T GROW UP in a church, I haven't found my faith or my Jesus in a place, and I won't sit here and preach to you. I'm not perfect, I cuss like a sailor, I lose my patience with people, I'm sassy, I'm stubborn, and I'm a sinner just like everyone else. Honestly, I've crossed Jesus more times than I can count.

I spent a lot of my life searching for where I might fit in my family, at school, outside of school, in my work, and even in church. And although most of the time, I didn't ever end up with exactly what I was looking for, I've learned one very big, loud, can't ignore it *lesson*.

There is a bigger plan and purpose for us.

I said earlier, make plans and God laughs. I believe that with everything I've got. From music, to healthcare, to new home sales, to sales management, training and coaching, and now dare I say author, I just won't accept that these moments in my life are random. Because they aren't.

My entire life has been a series of crazy God-winks.

I previously shared that I thought a God-wink was a phrase I made up. It wasn't until a few years ago that I shared the phrase in conversation with a beautiful human who told me there was an entire book dedicated to this idea! I couldn't believe it, but saw it as yet another sweet God-wink.

Whether this is the official definition or not, I consider a God-wink to be a moment in your day (life) when something so wonderfully timed happens that the only thing we can attribute it to is God's plan. I think of His "wink" to us like a little nudge from Heaven.

God-winks don't have to be a big grand gesture like a double rainbow in the sky driving to your last day of work while you bawl your eyes out wondering if you're making the right decision. But yes—that really did happen. They won't always be this way though. I've also had God-winks as slight as a text or phone call at the **exact** moment I needed them to happen.

Unfortunately, in the hustle, bustle, and shuffle of our day-to-day, God-winks are so easily overlooked. Why? Well, I think so many of us are waiting for that double rainbow when really, God-winks are all around us.

We just have to be willing to slow down long enough to see them. We may be asking for a sign, praying for direction, even crying out for it, but are we open to receiving it?

You know my favorite thing about God-winks? It's when we get to be the God-wink for someone else. It's right up there with loving people down.

I love giving love. I've shared this, but I really do mean it. If I had a dollar for every person who's said, "How did you know that I needed **this** right now?" or "You always reach out at exactly the right time," I'd be set for life.

These moments are anything from a text, a call, a silly gift, or small surprise, but I'm not out here wielding double rainbows.

My response is always the same. For whatever reason, I get these feelings pretty regularly where I now know God is clearly putting this person on my heart. On their receiving end, person after person has repeatedly claimed to me that it's always precisely the moment they needed it. Have you ever had that feeling too?

This isn't a coincidence. I definitely don't have a sixth sense. But it happens far too often in my life for my timing to be just that good. I assure you it's not; ask my husband. These are all God-winks.

Still unsure? Let me share one of my most favorite God-wink stories to date.

Despite not knowing, the day I would write this chapter, I woke up to a text from a sweet friend who had sent a couple of us the verse Matthew 5:16, "In the same way, you should be a light for other people. Live so that they will see the good things you do and praise your Father in Heaven."

What a beautiful way to start your day right?

During my writing process and to make sure I completed the book, I got into a really good rhythm. I'd work, pick up my daughter, enjoy our family time, and then once we wrapped up her bedtime, get to writing. This had been my routine for a few weeks without compromise.

That night while writing this chapter and during the **exact** moments that I was trying to generate my most favorite God-wink example, I received another text from a different friend sending me Matthew 5:16.

Mind you, before this, I had never read the verse, but here I was getting it twice in one day from two different people!

When I shared with her the phenomenon, do you know how she responded? ...*drumroll*... "God winks."

Mic drop.

Ah, I still get goosebumps! I responded with a screenshot telling her she wouldn't believe me but that at that very moment, I was typing the chapter on God-winks. Cue the goosebumps and waterworks because I began ugly crying all over myself. God is good, y'all.

For real, you can't deny that mic droppin' God-wink.

If you've still got your doubts, call me for a **bunch** of examples. ☺

Unapologetic Truth #14: Follow the Winks

The value in this is that when you're on the road to becoming Unapologetic, you have to believe your life has a bigger purpose. You have to know you were created to do something so wonderful and unique to **you**. This won't be the easy route, it won't always be clear, and it may not even make sense.

Heck, I'm writing this book right now wondering what in the world I'm doing. But the God-winks just keep rolling in and I won't deny them.

So you could spend years and years searching blindly on your own for your purpose, **or** you could lean into your God-winks and watch your story, purpose, and plan unfold. I hope you go with option two, I really do.

Because I can't wait to see that for not only you, but for the people around you and the people yet to be impacted by you.

> I wholeheartedly believe that spreading joy and sharing light is a sure way to hold on to our own. When we're open to giving, we also open ourselves up to receiving. So give the love, light, joy, and inspiration, as it will give itself right back to you.

The last note I'll leave you with is this…If you're looking for your own God-winks, your Jesus, or your direction, I would encourage you to consider looking in places you haven't looked before.

As an adult, I've realized that God speaks to me through music. After praying for an answer, direction, or peace, I'll wake up with a song on my heart that provides me clarity.

I'm sure music isn't the answer for all of us, but look for Him in your music, your art, your work, or your craft.

Maybe you hear him when you're hiking, walking, or driving with your windows down?

God isn't picky; he wants to meet you where you can find Him. But what I hope you'll consider is that God doesn't have to be found within the four walls of a building.

As important as this concept is for us, I think it's equally important to encourage our next generation to do the same. I wish I would've learned this a lot sooner in life, I may have found my God-winks a lot quicker.

> He's where we look for Him. He's where we listen for Him. He's where we open ourselves up to His plan and direction. So make sure you take the time to look for your own God-winks and your own direction.

• • •

Chapter Fifteen

Time and Jimbo

• • •

I TOLD Y'ALL I love big and loud. I do. I'm Unapologetic in how boldly I love. I'm quick to tell you that I love you, and on most days, I won't let strangers stay strangers. I do everything I can to be intentional, especially with those whose hearts I feel need it the most.

I love to give, I love to see people grow, and I love to feel like I left people a little better through loving on them.

I'll pat your arm, give you a hug, pay you a compliment, and help you find your superpower as a human. I try so hard to choose love whenever I can and I want you to know why. Because there is a big "why" and that same why has only grown stronger in the last fifteen years.

My dad, Jimmy, Jim, or Jimbo, taught me some really valuable lessons in life. I think a lot of our parents did (good and bad). As part of his legacy, now and always, I want to use this space to share them with you. His story has significantly shaped mine.

Jimbo served 27 years in the Illinois Army National Guard. He began his career as an E-1 Infantry Scout, spending 20 active-duty years and seven part-time Citizen Soldier years before retiring in 2012 as an Army Aviator, both Fixed and Rotary Wing rated.

My dad didn't come from much, was raised in a small Midwestern town, and after joining the military worked his way up from absolutely nothing. His final position was Chief Warrant Officer Five, Command Chief Warrant Officer for Illinois. He was the youngest in United States history to hold this rank. Not in his unit, not our state, but the entire nation.

My dad was extremely quiet, at least around us, humble, and hard-working. He put up with more crap than any one human ever should, but he never complained. He was admired, adored, and respected by those who knew him, worked with him, and worked for him.

Ironically enough, I didn't know any of this until I was 17 years old sitting at his retirement party. It was there that I watched one soldier after another, grown men and women, get to the podium to speak about my dad through tears and sniffles. Each recounted their own stories about how Chief Gaddis changed their life.

It was at this moment that I was humbled to learn that my dad not only served his country, but served everyone around him too. He was my first example of servant leadership. He went out of his way for the people who worked with him and was a natural innovator. His accomplishments form a mile-long list and although he shared them with hardly anyone, to know him was to be inspired by him.

Though for most of my childhood, I was provided a very different narrative.

My dad was gone a lot when I was little. He was a commercial pilot, working for the Guard, and flying privately. He stayed busy so that we could be free to do whatever we wanted. We weren't super close, but we weren't really allowed to be, either.

Much like the relationship I had with my sister, my dad and I were also pitted against each other for most of my life. You always had to pick a side at my house, and it was a lot easier to pick the side of the person who was home every single day.

The narrative that I was told was that my dad never wanted kids. That, and he definitely didn't want us. That's why he was always gone so much, or so we were told.

What I didn't realize as an adolescent was that when your occupation is a pilot along with being active duty, you're going to be gone a lot whether you want to be home or not. Unfortunately, six-year-old me didn't know better. This isn't a rebuttal you come up with when you're told repeatedly that your dad doesn't want you. Instead, you accept it as the truth. And maybe he didn't want kids, but here we are.

Despite whether he wanted us or not, my dad never failed to provide for us. He worked tirelessly to allow us to do whatever, be whoever, and aspire to whatever we wanted to be.

If we needed music lessons, we had the instruments and the instructors. When we wanted acting careers, he drove us to Chicago for acting classes. When we wanted to compete, there was never a hesitation to get us whatever we needed. My mom executed our dreams that my dad was investing in. He's the reason "The Price of Peace" got sponsored in the first place. It was funded all from a conversation he had on a flight.

There was never a dream too big or an idea too silly. But in a primarily one-income household, I wonder as an adult how much of a financial strain all of this put on our family. Although I've never directly asked how much our hobbies, big ideas, crazy dreams, and endless music endeavors cost our family, I do know that my dad was always working.

My dad worked extremely hard. He sacrificed a lot so that the people around him didn't have to. I admired him for this and still do. BUT he spent a great deal of his life working and sacrificing only to be forced into retirement by a diagnosis that robs him each day of mobility and time. This leads me to the first official Jimbo lesson.

Jimbo Lesson One:

Work hard, but don't work your life away.

Most of us are drowning in a culture that promotes burnout and sacrificing ourselves for our careers, organizations, or the next promotion. Top achievers and high performers are being raked over the coals rather than valued and supported.

Companies are taking advantage of those willing to do "whatever it takes" to hit the target, meet the goal, or achieve that KPI. But at what cost?

My dad climbed the ranks from a very young age and made a significant impact throughout his career. He broke records, won awards, and achieved a ranking no one else at his age had, but received a diagnosis of Parkinson's disease just a few months later.

He worked tirelessly his entire life, all to have it taken away from him in a mere moment. Everything he had accomplished, wiped away from him at no fault of his own. A diagnosis completely outside of his own control, yet it would control him from each day on.

Can you imagine?

We work so hard, but for what?

We skip some of life's greatest moments for careers that ultimately mean nothing at the end of the day. For it's not our titles that make up our legacy; it's the people we've impacted along the way.

So I'm begging you—don't sacrifice yourself, your dreams, your daughter's soccer game, your son's senior concert, or your anniversary for a job.

We are replaceable everywhere else but home.

Any Alabama fans reading this? (Roll Tide!) Nick Saban coached football at the University of Alabama for 17 seasons with a winning percentage of .878.

After announcing his retirement, do you know how long it took for them to replace him? An absolute legend? 48 hours. We are replaceable everywhere else but home.

I'll be honest, I struggle with this personally. I have a hard time setting boundaries and turning it off. But when I really get sucked into the vortex, I remind myself that we aren't guaranteed do-overs for any of these things. We aren't promised anything in this life. I remind myself of Jimbo's story.

A fantastic sermon said once, "Are you living to die? Or dying to live?" I think you should ask yourself those same questions.

Jimbo Lesson Two:

Time is not guaranteed. In fact, it's the only finite resource and can't be replenished or regained once it's spent.

I briefly shared earlier that my dad has Parkinson's disease (PD) and if you're not aware, it's a neurodegenerative disease without a cure. It absolutely sucks and unless you too have a diagnosis of PD, you really can't understand. His "good" time is not guaranteed, his body stops working more each day, and the challenges he has faced before even turning 60 are just unfair.

Don't try telling Jimmy this though; he doesn't let anything slow him down, including his depletion of dopamine.

So are you ready for the good news after all that? No one defines your very next moment but you. Choose joy, choose life, choose love, and choose to live. Because right now, you have that choice.

I challenge you to love loud, love big, and live fully while you can because you never know when it can all change.

I also encourage you to maintain this perspective when the going gets tough. Attitude is everything.

This is exactly why I don't leave anything on the table and refuse to walk away from a conversation with anything left unsaid.

Some people love me for it and some will never truly understand my why, which leads me to our last lesson.

Jimbo Lesson Three:

Stop judging people. For real, y'all—whether it's in person or online, stop.

You never, and I mean never, know what someone is going through. Treat others with kindness, show grace, and be patient because none of us are immune in this life and you never know what version of hard life may hit you with next. We've seen it firsthand.

For my dad, on top of having a body that's working against him, it often seems like the world can be too. I'll never forget the first time I got confronted in public about what was "wrong" with my dad.

We were at Talladega, my dad had just walked down the bleachers for a drink, and the guy sitting in the row in front of us turned around and said with an accent so thick I could barely make it out, "What is wrong with him?"

Y'all, if you want to see Jerry Springer's hottest but never-aired episode, come at me about my dad.

Newsflash, there is nothing wrong with him. I have all but lost my Jesus with people at races, concerts, bars, and restaurants. While my dad can brush it off, I find the nearest pedestal. The stares, whispers, comments, and discrimination got so outrageous that my sassy-Cassy self decided to make business cards for him.

These were meant to be communication cards that he could have on hand when he needed them. You can see it below.

Medical Alert: Education Card

I have PARKINSON'S DISEASE which often times causes shakiness and jerkiness.

Public places, large crowds, along with ongoing observation from strangers can impact the effectiveness and timeliness of my medication.

Thank you for your time and understanding.
Feel free to buy me a drink!

-Jimmy, 14-years living with PD and still feisty as ever

For more information on
Parkinson's Disease visit
www.parkinson.org

What I love even more than these cards is the fact that Jimmy hands them out. These are far more effective than me confronting people one by one, which I did with zero problems. This route just makes my dad a lot less uncomfortable. And of course, a free drink or two from a new friend every now and then doesn't hurt either.

I recognize that it could always be worse. I know this and I repeat this to myself a lot. Both my bonus mom (definitely more than a "stepmom") and dad have made the choice to live their lives to the absolute fullest. My bonus mom brings out the greatest joy in my dad. She has revived his inner kid again. Seeing him so happy is ultimately what matters.

I'm also not perfect, so being the sassy, stubborn, want to know-it-all/fix-it-all/cure-it-all human, I struggle with not being able to control how Jimmy chooses to spend his time. I'll admit it, Dad, if you're reading this, I'm still working on it.

If you have a family member undergoing a challenging diagnosis, it's so hard to be a quiet bystander. So even though I don't always agree with their choices and wish things were different, through a great deal of counseling and intentionality, I choose to make my peace with that every day.

But selfishly, for me and my family, I want more time. I want him to be here for as much as possible, as long as possible, and as the Jimbo we know and love.

Feeling this way is okay, but accepting that it's not within your control is equally as important, simply to protect your own peace and mental health.

The big thing to remember is if someone is struggling, spare your judgments and don't assume. If someone needs help, be the helper. If you have the opportunity to show kindness or give love, freaking give it. It's as easy as that.

Unapologetic Truth #15: Love and Live Now

We all have complicated relationships with our loved ones. Whether it's our parents, siblings, children, or all of the above—navigating our families can be challenging.

There also isn't a person or family out there who hasn't faced a crippling diagnosis or a heartbreaking loss.

We all have a story, and we all know someone impacted.

What I find to be so different family to family, person to person, situation to situation is how we choose to show up **after** this.

Although my relationship with my dad remains complicated, I am so grateful that through my parents' divorce and his diagnosis, I really got to know him. I learned so much from him and his example, as a person, as a father, and as a servant leader.

I admired him, looked up to him, and strived to work as hard as he did, but it wasn't until college when we had time just the two of us, that I realized how selfless he'd been for my family.

It was also when I became brutally aware of these lessons.

Childhood drama and trauma aside—I always appreciated my dad, but I wish I knew then what I know now.

I wasted a lot of time being bitter, one-sided, and resentful. I wasted a lot of time I didn't know I wouldn't have.

But regardless of how it started out, I'm so grateful for the intentional time we've had since then.

So what?

Prioritize the people around you over everything else.

Don't wait for a diagnosis, health scare, or loss to be your starting point to living an intentional life.

Never let anyone or anything ever make you question how or why you show up as your most Unapologetic Self.

Lastly, Jimbo, I wouldn't be where I am if it wasn't for your example. I am so proud to be your daughter.

• • •

Part Three

Warning:

I've shared a lot with you about the work I'm doing, what I've been through, what I've learned, and where I hope to go.

But as we shift into the remaining chapters of the book, I have to caution you, it's almost your turn.

It's just about time for you to own your journey.

Are you ready?

Chapter Sixteen

Failing is Just Learning the Hard Way

• • •

Y'ALL, I'M A BIG FAT FAILURE. Truly. I'm so bad at so many things.

Don't believe me?

Quick list:

- Sports: absolutely not
- Cooking: have you cooked an onion without peeling it? Well, I have.
- Baking: I burn it or your money back
- Math: You can find me counting on my fingers to calculate the tip after Taco Tuesday
- One-liners and phrases: I will mess it up, every time.
- Short-term memory: I write it down, or it's lost forever.

The list goes on and on, but have you ever lost at something that you will never in your life forget?

Random fact about me, I hate losing.

I'm an awful loser.

Doesn't matter if it's for the million-dollar jackpot or a simple board game, your girl here does not like to lose.

Don't believe me? We could ask my father-in-law about a four-hour game of Risk that I brutally lost. It was rough for all of those involved. I'm still embarrassed and haven't played the game since.

BUT the loss that just really grinds my gears was the summer before I started seventh grade. I had not yet learned that *failing is just learning the hard way*. Keep in mind that this is a working concept for many of us.

I was competing at the fair dressed as a 1950s service woman. I sang a military mash-up that, if I do say so myself, was just off the charts. I felt fantastic about my performance.

Despite thinking that I'd just earned myself a one-way ticket to first place, I lost the competition to a teeny-bopper karate kid. This girl was not even five or six years old and came out wearing a white karate outfit (gi) with her colored belt, throwing kicks, "Hi-Yas!" and won first place. I was astonished—stunned! Oh, and pissed.

I'm not ashamed to admit that I still hold some slightly bitter feelings toward this experience.

Was she cute? Absolutely. Would I call it top-tier talent? Hardly. Sorry to this probably now terrific human, but it felt a bit off. If you're thinking, "Cassy, you sound like a sore loser," you're right and I know.

Unfortunately for me, this was only the beginning of losses, especially in the music sector. I continued to lose. A lot, a lot. You'd think that losing time and time again would desensitize me to it, but it didn't. My attitude at the time was immature and despite my age, I had a lot of evolving to do when it came to how I handled losing.

I share this though because recognizing how we handle loss holds importance for all of us. We have to give ourselves grace in this space of growth, learning, and healing.

If you still struggle with losing like I do or even often opt out of an opportunity because you're fearful of losing, you've found your space. I'm so glad you're here.

Luckily or unluckily for me (depending on who you ask, I guess), even at a very young age, I was too much of a high "achiever" to stop trying. That, mixed with a fierce amount of stubbornness, and I kept going back for more.

My losing trend continued and as a young adult, I kept on failing, or at least that's what it felt like.

My first big failure though was our music career slowly crumbling around us. It's always hard to not feel like a failure when it doesn't go as we hoped or planned. I was only 19 when we decided it was time to walk away and called it quits.

"The Price of Peace," Chasing Hope, and our military kids and their families had been our life for several years. Touring, writing, performing, speaking, and inspiring, it was something we thought we'd be able to do forever.

When you truly believe that you're Making a Difference, where do you go from that?

How do you "beat" something that feels like the top of the summit?

So there we were. Our parents were getting divorced, our music career was over, and our lives were falling apart.

Cue up the "low point" in my best Kate Winslet accent (again, watch *The Holiday* if you haven't!).

Amid trying to be a full-time student and musician, I was actively failing in the second program I thought was meant for me. I struck out with my music business major and was on to pursuing my place in the physician assistant program.

It was during my sophomore year that chemistry really handed me my you-know-what. We had a class of almost 200 students and a professor who had an extremely difficult time communicating with us due to a language barrier. We were rocking a D average as a whole and for most of us, the only reason it was a D and not an F was because of the lab attached to it.

During a vent session in the one class I loved, public speaking, my professor asked me if I'd ever considered exploring a major in communication disorders. After a conversation with Eric's aunt who is a speech-language pathologist, I felt like I had a new, viable option.

At this point, my college advisor and I were officially buds. I switched majors officially for the third time. Third time's a charm, right?

The Communication Disorders Program (CDIS) was small, with only 18 of us in the program. Not only would we follow the normal academic calendar, but we would also have clinical assignments, as we were the only undergraduate program in the state to have our own speech clinic.

I had no idea that some of the very best pioneers of our industry were professors in our program.

Remember when I thought chemistry handed my ass to me? I hadn't had phonetics and language acquisition yet. In the voice of Kevin Hart, "She wasn't ready." Because she (me) was not.

Cue the seventh-grade beating by the karate kid. The feelings that prior loss had caused me were nothing compared to the CDIS program at MTSU.

Let the good "fails" roll. I was humbled by my first semester in that program.

Humbled.

These courses were some of the hardest classes I'd ever had. It was like learning a foreign language but in English, which honestly made it even worse. I'm also not an easy study. Some of y'all have been blessed to be academically gifted. Your girl here was not.

I had to **work** for it. I practically revived the notecard industry, making more flashcards than any one human should. These were the days before Quizlet, so I hand wrote them all. I even went as far as using different colored pens because I could picture them in color when test time came. Anyone else use that strategy?

I didn't have much of an option. It was studying this or, well, I wouldn't pass. If you can relate, don't take any shortcuts. It really is worth the grind. Those "A's" look even prettier on our paper, I promise you that.

I was so fortunate by the amount of grace given to me by my professors, classmates, and even random strangers who consoled me on whatever blue bench was open at the time.

My classmates and I studied our butts off. I had never made so many study guides, flashcards, or cheat sheets. Little did I know, pursuing my master's degree would make this look like a walk in the park. But my goodness, my time in the CDIS program taught me the importance of discipline, practice, and persistence on a completely new level.

Looking back, we can all appreciate that our professors were doing what they could to prepare us for exactly how hard the real world would be just before we were submerged in it.

I eventually found my footing, my place, and my elephant sound.

After two and a half years, I made it through this exceptional program, all while dealing with my parents' divorce.

I was feeling like a million bucks about my clinical performance, grades, my GRE score, and how I was concluding my undergraduate degree. What I wasn't ready for was being **denied** admission into graduate school with my peers.

Fun fact for you: One cannot practice as a speech therapist without a master's degree. An undergraduate degree is a stepping stone (step one of two) to becoming a speech therapist.

Sure, some states allow licensure for a speech assistant, but if you wanted your CCC (Certificate of Clinical Competence) you had to obtain a graduate degree along with completing your clinical fellowship year. You couldn't do either of these without your master's degree in speech-language pathology.

Despite my losing track record, I couldn't have prepared myself for this failure. It felt like the ultimate slap in the face. I'd been through so much over those four years and when I didn't think it could get any more complicated, it did.

So when I didn't get in alongside so many of my friends, I made an emotional and impulsive decision to move to Florida and dragged Eric with me.

You can cue my downward spiral right here. Similar to sixth-grade me along with fourteen-year-old me, this was a phase where I just kept falling (and failing) further and further away from who I wanted to be.

So in my attempt to control the only thing I could, after four years of long distance, a lot of ups and downs, breakups, comebacks, and adventure, Eric and I moved to Florida together away from everything we knew and loved.

The move to Florida was made possible with my dad's help. Eric took a job working with a landscaping company. The job he agreed to did not end up being the job he found himself in. We learned quickly that he detested the work and the heat.

I was working for a private practice getting some exposure to clinical work, but primarily handling their billing and prior authorizations. This job was a huge blessing and I am still so grateful to the family who owned the company.

Despite enjoying my job, Eric and I found ourselves in the land of snowbirds. It was practically impossible to find people our own age, let alone friends. So we spent a lot of time going out and putting a Band-Aid on this very weird transition in our lives.

Ultimately, Eric and I fell on our face. I take the blame for a lot of it. Our relationship broke in this chapter of life like it had never broken before. But by the grace of God, here we stand.

After a very long nine months in Florida, Eric was offered the opportunity to move back to Iowa to take a coaching position. In hindsight, I really should've let him go on his own. He didn't necessarily invite me to go, but he also didn't tell me to stay.

Since I followed him there, I applied to graduate school at the same university and it was there that I finally got in, and as an early admission. I couldn't believe it.

After a year off and wondering if I'd ever get into graduate school, I not only got in, but I was one of the first select few to be admitted. The stars were finally aligning, or so I thought.

One month before my graduate program started, Eric and I broke up. It was messy, awful, and absolutely heartbreaking. I hit a level of "failure" I never even knew possible. Losing Eric might've been like losing everything—at least that's what it felt like.

So there I was in Iowa, alone, without friends or family, committed to a graduate program that I couldn't afford to move forward without.

It was at this point that I was throwing up the big "why me?" pity party and begging for not just a God-wink, but a life preserver ring because I was drowning.

Luckily for me, I got two of them—their names are Tori and Amanda. And I believe, with all my heart, that the only reason I was trapped in Iowa, away from everything and everyone important to me, was to meet two of my life's greatest friends.

During this time, I became my most invincible self. I'd lost my family, I'd lost Eric, I'd lost the Williamsons, and I had been stripped of literally everything I knew to be good in my life.

So not only did I become invincible, but I also became the ugliest version of "me." Not only did I have to become strong like I'd never been before, but in my heartbreak and bitterness, I got mean. I won't say I was like this all the time or to everyone. I had my moments.

But as I shared earlier, my "highs are high" and my "lows are low." I lost friends, I had some radically crazy moments, and I burned bridges where I didn't necessarily need to do so. None of which I pride myself on.

I'm thankful to have come out of those two years on the other side. I'm extremely grateful to the professors, friends, and family who carried me through that time. I'm also proud to say that with a lot of grace and counseling, I learned a great deal about myself from those experiences.

So as I moved out and away from Iowa, I promised myself to take those lessons with me. Although getting my master's in speech-language pathology was and still is a huge accomplishment, I look at this time in my life as one of my biggest failures.

I had lost myself again. I let the "darkness" surrounding me take away so much of my light and who I was.

★ Fortunately for me, during each failure, lesson, and challenging moment throughout my life, I was always given someone exceptional. Someone who poured into me and gave me the inspiration I so desperately needed to push forward and try again. So I did.

Unapologetic Truth #16: Rise Through Failure

Looking back, all of the losses were really good for me. They've shaped me, strengthened me, and supported my bigger purpose.

Whether we lose to the karate kid or experience failure and loss in a much bigger way, we have to embrace these moments in our lives as opportunities to learn, grow, and adapt.

Failure is really just learning the hard way, right?

Questions to reflect on:

- What can our losses teach us?
- What can our failures guide us through or to?
- Is there a person there at the bottom we wouldn't have seen otherwise?
- Is there a light in the midst of the darkness that we could've only found after the storm?

This chapter was incredibly hard for me to write and I couldn't even bear to share it all with you. I'm not one to jump up and down about my weaknesses. It doesn't light me up to share my losses with you.

I told you I don't like losing and I still don't.

You want to know the best part about losing, falling, and failing the hard way? These seasons in our life are only temporary. None of these moments have lasted forever. Although there were times when I didn't know how I'd get through, I always did.

Every time I look back at these moments, I'm reminded that from every loss, time and time again, I grew stronger, braver, more resilient, and ready for whatever adventure I'd be facing next.

I hope and pray that you will see the same in your own life.

I'm no longer scared of failing. I may not like losing, but I'm not afraid of failing. I'd challenge you to work toward the same mindset.

Be willing to lose, leap, fall, and fail **because** *failure is just learning the hard way, after all.*

• • •

Chapter Seventeen

Asking for Help

• • •

WHEW, BUCKLING MYSELF UP because this one's a toughie.

Now that we've beaten the "failing" discussion with a stick, I can't think of a better time to talk about asking for help.

Anybody else have a big ole bucket full of pride?

I know I do.

Whether it's being a perfectionist, a people pleaser, type A, high achiever, one of those, some of those, or all of those—it is really freaking hard to raise that hand and ask for help.

It's not just me, right?

After a pretty heavy conversation with a dear friend, I was reminded that asking for help is a critical component of embracing the road to being Unapologetic.

Although we've talked a great deal about the adversity you'll likely face on this journey, the support you'll need along the way, and finding your tribe, it was during this specific conversation that I had a true epiphany.

We can have the greatest tribe of people on the planet, but if we don't know how to ask for help or be vulnerable, our friends are only as impactful as we let them be. We don't know what we don't know.

With work, kids, fur babies, spouses, family, you name it, life is speeding right by, and a great deal of people are just making it. I know that there are periods of my life that I feel as though I'm surviving, not thriving. This makes it extremely easy for life to blast right by us.

As much as we love our friends and want to be there for them, unless they're sending a 911 text or SOS call, it's easy to blink and weeks or months have gone by. I know I'm guilty of this even with as intentional as I try to be.

Really, unless I have that feeling I talked to y'all about, the God-wink nudge, most days I'm a hamster running on the wheel of toddler-wife-working-mom-chaos.

Even though I love every bit of my life, it's all-consuming when you're in the thick of it. If you know, you know. It definitely hasn't always been this way and it won't last forever. But it is why I strongly believe that having friendships as adults is so much harder to maintain.

This is nothing to be ashamed of; it's real life for so many of us. So what?

If we know this, if we feel this, then we also have to recognize that our friends cannot be our lifelines if we aren't asking them to be. This deep-end friend that I referenced earlier was in the thick of some really big, heavy "life" stuff. As she shared with me what was happening, we were both speaking through broken phrases and tears.

She needed a friend. She desperately needed a lifeline, but I was not aware of to what degree until that call.

Believe me or not, the only reason I could be there for her at that exact moment was because I had a God-wink nudge the week prior to set up a virtual date. It was then (and probably only then) that she was able to open up to me for love and support.

When we began to discuss who she could lean on in her inner circle, she shared with me how hard it is to ask for help.

Isn't that the truth?

I feel as though we are inhibited by our own guilt of "dumping" our problems, challenges, or adversity on someone else, especially when we know they are facing their own challenges.

> Despite what we've been taught or conditioned to believe, I have to tell you, we shouldn't have to do the hard stuff alone. And honestly, we can't sustain it.

So how do we change this narrative?

The first step starts with **you**.

Many of us have been conditioned to believe that if we ask for help, whether in a personal or professional setting, we'll be considered weak, incapable, or unable.

To compound that, we've also been taught to believe that showing emotions is a sign of weakness or classifies us as "emotional." So add that on to also worrying about "dumping" our problems on others and we have the perfect trifecta of why it's often easier to suffer alone.

I'm going to call bullshit right now and say that speaking to, out, and about your weaknesses is not a weakness at all. "The first step is admitting you have a problem."

I mean, come on—we cannot navigate our way through life, reach our full potential, and find our way to being Unapologetically Ourselves without being able to lean into the people (world) around us.

★ I recognize that asking for help will most definitely look different on different people, but the principle here remains the same. Whether you're experiencing burnout at work, struggling to get through the day, or dealing with a situation where you desperately need a friend, all of these situations are opportunities for you to lean into someone whom you trust to help you through it.

It's extremely important to know yourself here and do a temperature check. I shared with you that I feel my feelings in a big way—I do. So for me, it's imperative that I keep a pulse on ME at all times. Especially now, as a mom, it's more important than ever. This skill was not something I could do 10 years ago and I'm going to call it emerging as short as five years ago.

I use the word skill deliberately because it is just that. Being able to self-reflect on how you're doing, specifically when things are challenging, is something we all need to be working toward when fighting to be our very best selves.

How do we do this? I won't play counselor here, because I'm not. But I'm more than happy to share with you what's worked for me. I'm a ball of stress and anxiety most of the time. Functioning and fighting, remember?

On most days, I can manage my own emotions or cope with daily stress by talking out loud with Eric, my friends, or a co-worker. Maybe not every single day, but the "get it off your chest" so to speak. That's Phase 1 for me of "check yourself before you wreck yourself." We can call this daily maintenance, like brushing your teeth, stress edition.

Phase 2 is going to be actually asking someone for help. Not just a quick vent session to get it out there, but an actual ask. Phase 2 is when you're starting to feel as though you're approaching that "tip over" point, but you're tagging someone in. You can feel yourself beginning to struggle, and you're course correcting early on.

It could be something as simple or easy as delegating a task to a colleague or leaning on your spouse for support with a chore at home. Kudos to those who are already implementing their own version of Phase 2! Work smarter, not harder.

Phase 3 is when you've waited too long to ask, be it out of stubbornness or necessity. Either way, you've now become emotional. Whether you're crying because you're upset, displaying a short fuse because you're frustrated, stress cleaning anything that comes within two feet of you, or combining them all (my speciality area)—this is the danger zone.

Picture me crying because I'm so mad while frantically cleaning everything around me. This phase for me is like waiting too long to eat. Just like that Snickers commercial, "You're not you when you're hungry." I'm not me in Phase 3.

For me, I really can't reset in this phase until I've found my "Snickers."

What does that look like? I'll give you a few examples that I've tapped into more times than I'd like to admit.

- Calling a friend asking them for an emergency lunch date

- Scheduling a babysitter so you and your spouse can get out and away together
- Taking a personal day off and away from work so you can reset
- Going for a long walk outside
- Putting on your Feel-Good Jesus playlist while sitting in the sun
- Cleaning up the space around you

The idea here is to ask yourself, "What is going to help me get to the other side in this moment of struggle and fill my cup back up?" This will look different for each of us, but the important part is knowing what serves you in these moments.

That leads me to the last phase, Phase 4.

When I cannot manage myself through daily maintenance, friends and family, or by taking some time off to reset, I recognize through doing a temperature check on myself that it's time to bring out the big guns.

This is often when I'm not sleeping, I'm having a hard time focusing, my anxiety is reeling, and I'm not finding the normal joy in the everyday things that make me happy. I'm agitated, tired, and easily upset. I know that once I've hit Phase 4, it's time to book some time with my counselor.

It's there that I find out at a deeper level what needs to change in the current space I'm in to get myself back to baseline. What has changed in my life that has gotten me to this place? I will be functioning and fighting for the rest of my life. The important part here is that I will never give up. I will never stop fighting. I hope you never do either.

Let me remind you that these are just my phases and I do not execute them perfectly. As I've become more aware of my challenges and triggers, I've set myself up for success proactively.

During phases of life where I know I'm going to face more adversity, I keep myself in counseling regularly to make sure I have someone holding me accountable to all the good work I've done.

But, for a long time, Eric was the only one holding me accountable. Bless that man for all the reasons. There was a point where I was bringing my homework back to him and asking him to call me out on my bullshit when I needed him to. Thank goodness he did and still does.

The biggest thing to remember throughout all of this is to value progress over perfection. I'm so far from perfect it's not even funny, but I have come a long way from where I started, and I celebrate the great deal of progress I have made.

But real talk, y'all, I wouldn't be able to keep a straight face if I had to tell you that I'm over here acting as a "super self-reflector" who's got it together all the time. I do not.

What I do have is a very loving group of people around me who know what's important to me, which includes taking care of my mental health, breaking the cycle of generational trauma, showing up for my family from a place of love, and being my very best Unapologetic Self.

We cannot consistently check in on ourselves, get what we need, and be the very best spouse, friend, and parent, child, employee etc. without asking for help.

Even moreso, not only can we not pour from an empty cup, but what are we doing to refill our tank all the way up? When most of us are always running somewhere between half a tank and E (empty), we only deplete ourselves of what we need that much faster.

So I'll say again, what are you doing to lean into those around you so that you can be your very best self?

Unapologetic Truth #17: Boundaries Build Bridges

For a long time this felt self-centered to me. I was also raised in an environment where this was often labeled "selfish." That's also the word I'm called most by certain members of my family. So for a long time, I would've much rather sacrificed myself than "inconvenience" someone around me.

What do you think?

Does this sound or feel selfish to you?

If you answered "yes," why?

Why does this feel self-centered?

Consider reflecting on why it feels this way for you.

Trust me, I can relate to that feeling. I've had to work through that myself. Asking for help, leaning into other people around us, doing what it takes for us to support ourselves isn't a weakness and it's most definitely not selfish. But keep in mind that boundaries are frequently called both of these things by those attempting to control or manipulate us.

I talk to people all the time who give, give, give, oh and give some more without a pause or second thought. Most of the time, these same individuals are also really struggling. They are burned out, physically, mentally, and emotionally exhausted, and teetering on the edge of unhappiness. I've been one of these people.

When you're in this place, you aren't prioritizing exercise, eating habits, sleep, mindfulness, gratitude practices, or breaks from the screen. You're living in "hero mode," ready to drop whatever it is you may be doing to help or get the job done. And man, it can be rough. I still fight this uphill battle with myself.

What I've come to find through my own experiences and talks with the people around me is a hard truth. This way of life is absolutely exhausting and we can't pour from an empty cup. We can't serve or fulfill our life's purpose running on E.

> If you've got big dreams, but no boundaries in place, keep dreaming—because that's all they'll be.

If this feels harsh to you, good. It should. If asking for help is your forte and you might as well wear the badge that says "delegation master," then just skip on right ahead. BUT if you find yourself reading this and relating to what we're talking about, please spend some time on the questions below and use them as ONLY a starting point, recognizing that there's much greater work to be done.

1. Who do you trust to lean on in moments of hardship? I'd like you to answer twice:
    1. Personally
    2. Professionally
2. What is a "stuck" in your life that you could make "unstuck" by asking for help from this person or someone else?
3. Brainstorm a list of things here that fill your cup when you need a reset
4. What would a temperature check look like on you?
5. What are some of your signs that it's time to ask for help?
6. Who in your life do you feel could benefit from your support that you can practice this exercise with? (It takes a village—I challenge you to be the *village* for someone around you.)

• • •

Chapter Eighteen

Growing Away from Comparison

• • •

WE DON'T ALWAYS LOVE the card we're dealt, or maybe even the hand.

Some of us have a much easier journey than others and it's almost impossible in the world we live in now not to play the comparison game. It's challenging to avoid throwing ourselves a pity party when the going gets tough. It's especially difficult to keep pushing forward when everyone around you appears to be thriving.

But not everyone is thriving. Not everyone has it as together as they appear. And most of us are just figuring it out as we go.

Much like the choices we've already mentioned, we also **CHOOSE** the narrative we tell others.

We **CHOOSE** and dictate the story from what we share with the people around us all the way to what we post on social media.

Some are more raw, vulnerable, and open. They'll share the good, the bad, and the ugly. Others will only unveil what they think is "worthy" of sharing.

Why am I telling you this?

Because when you're struggling in the space that you're in, it's really easy to forget this. You begin to spiral, comparing your life to the perception of what you see around you. You neglect to look at what IS going right and focus solely on what your life is lacking.

It's all a big scheme to pull you down deeper and further into the rabbit hole. Do not let yourself get stuck there.

I'm definitely not compromising on my honesty now that we've made it this far. So in full transparency, I still have to remind myself, too frequently, not to compare my life or journey to anyone else's. This is not easy!

Especially when someone is posting about their seventh vacation that year and you're stuck staring out your window while a torrential downpour is taking place outside. At that moment, I might as well be "Sadness" from *Inside Out* because "Woe is me."

I've come a very long way in this journey, but every now and then you can still catch me saying, "well that's just my luck" or "that's our luck" because it really does feel like we've just got a broken deck of cards. And when I say "we," I mean unfortunately my sister is in the same boat and I've rubbed off on Eric too.

> But I'm not kidding...It really feels like our family didn't carry our own Madame Zeroni up the mountain.

If there's going to be a person who gets blasted from the sky with bird poop, it'll be me (and it will somehow be caught on camera). Flat tire, random rainstorm with no umbrella, slowest grocery line, cockroach crawling on your arm but not anyone else's while minding your own business in the hot tub, you name it…It's me.

I jokingly blame kissing too many stingrays. On a cruise in the seventh grade, our tour guide told us during an excursion with the stingrays that kissing one would give us seven years good luck. I did the quick math, made a plan, and kissed several stingrays, thinking that I just set myself up for life. Joke's on me!! I'm one unlucky penny.

But in all seriousness, I truly am blessed where it counts. Look at this amazing journey I've gotten to take with you.

We choose our outcomes, always.
We create our own success story.
No one else.

As we navigate a shift from comparison to gratitude, it's essential you recognize if this is a "problem area" for you first. Is it?

I have several people in my life who do not envy, who do not compare, and who spend little to no time even observing what other people are doing. Bless them!

I also know people who live in spaces of insecurity and are consumed by what others are doing. They live to compare and inhibit their own growth wasting time engrossing themselves in the lives of others.

I'd ask yourself a few questions:

- Where do you fall on the comparison spectrum?
- How much time do you spend growing yourself?

- How much time do you spend watching the growth around you?

From there, growth starts with you. And growth, development, and big shifts in your life are all nourished by a mindset of positivity and gratitude.

We are so fortunate to be in a time where we don't have to reinvent the wheel on this concept. You can explore gratitude journals, daily gratitude apps, and even daily inspiration feeds that provide short prompts to initiate your own thoughts on gratitude. This is my nice way of telling you that there are no excuses for not jumping into some sort of practice!

★ For us to effectively grow away from comparison, we have to find the good happening in our own lives. There will be seasons where this is clear and other times when you have to dig deep, but it's no different than carving out time for physical exercise. Sometimes it's easy, sometimes it takes all you have just to get there.

You get to choose your hard, so pick something that serves your growth and your progress.

Unapologetic Truth #18:
Give Thanks for the Journey

Much like the choices we've already talked about, it's a conscious effort you have to make every day to be Unapologetically You and celebrate exactly where you are in your journey.

Not only where you are, but also where this road is leading you to.

So as you navigate these efforts and map out your next steps, ask:

- How are you currently showing up for yourself, if at all?
- How are you practicing gratitude each day?
- What will you do to hold yourself accountable over time?

Let's tap back into our village as needed on this one, because you'll likely want an accountability partner as you get started. I put this on my Eric tab when I started out and he still calls me out when I get in a negative headspace.

Although gratitude looks different for everyone, if you aren't spending five minutes a day (at least) practicing a grateful heart, you will chain yourself to negativity without realizing you're even doing so.

We can always find something to be thankful for; we're here, aren't we?

• • •

Chapter Nineteen

The Road to My Better Half

• • •

> Y'all have to know how long I kept kicking the can of this chapter down the road. I couldn't stop crying long enough to write whenever I got to Eric and I can't kick the can any longer. Let's do this.

I WANT TO OPEN with vulnerability and honesty to keep with the trend. Whatever love story of rainbows and sunshine you've painted in your head for Eric and me based on what you've read thus far, please know that amid all of the things that make our story my favorite, our story also holds its own hurricane season, a few tornadoes, and a tsunami or two.

Sarcasm aside, Eric's and my relationship is by far my life's greatest gift, but I will not bullshit you here by saying that it's been a walk in the park. Just like every other love story, our relationship comes with some dark days, obstacles, adversity, and challenges too.

When you start dating at 14, you're not prepared to fight for a relationship for the rest of your life, but I told y'all I love big, and Eric was no exception. I went all in.

Throughout high school and college, Eric and I broke up on more than one occasion. Whether it was over the push to be single, fighting long distance, or just being tired of how hard it was to be in such a long-term relationship at such a young age, parts of our journey were a hot mess. People got in the way, places kept us apart, and life threw me a lot of really grown-up curveballs that I don't blame Eric for wanting to take a break from.

To the girls who tried to get in our way during this time, and there were a lot of them, I'm really not sorry for fighting like hell for the only light I had in my life. They probably didn't know the darkness I was fighting, just like I didn't know theirs either. That version of me was crazy in every way. Remember Jerry Springer? I was holding on to hope the only way I knew how (by being mean).

During graduate school, or what I'll call "hurricane season," I latched onto a group of friends who only knew a version of me without Eric. I'd argue that was not only one of the hardest times in my life, but one of the worst versions of me as a result. I'm extremely grateful for the two humans who stood by me in spite of how I acted during that time. Deep-end friends turned lifers.

In the fall of 2015, my best friend and I moved to Nashville for a 12-week clinical placement. This was also when I decided that I really needed to cut Eric out of my life and attempt to move on. Up until that point, we had never given ourselves a clean break and I knew that the physical distance would be my only chance.

Eric had broken my heart the year prior and after what I'd consider to be our true breakup, we'd never really gotten back together. Eric was ready, but I wasn't, especially since I was moving states away, yet again.

Our lives were also going in two very different directions personally and professionally. Every friend around me was encouraging me to give myself a chance to be on my own, so I did. What an absolute dumpster fire that was.

Y'all, I know some people choose to date around. I know many people are happy on their own. But as someone who hadn't really had to date their entire life, it's rough out there on those streets.

This was the era of Tinder and Bumble and my goodness, it's not for the faint of heart. The roller coaster ride that was "dating"...whew.

I have to thank the Cubs for winning the World Series in 2016 for saving me from myself and resuscitating Eric and my relationship.

If you didn't know, prior to 2016, the Cubs had not won a World Series since 1908. This was a big deal. My friend and I were forced to watch the entire series in Spanish because it's all our TV network had at the time. We made the best of it, but as a Cubs fan (and loser), I knew what this win would mean to the Williamsons. When they won, all I could think about was Eric.

The day after they won, I was driving to clinicals when the song "Woke Up in Nashville" by Seth Ennis came on and the tears just started flowing. That song along with the Cubs World Series win were the God-winks I needed to swallow my pride and reach out to Eric after several long weeks of no communication.

I have to share that throughout this time, Eric reached out to me, and I ignored him. He says this was when I broke his heart—a few tornadoes. I still regret being so ugly to him, but at the time, I felt like the only option I had was a clean break.

Luckily in true Eric fashion, he showed me grace and loyalty that I didn't deserve. So when I reached out to him that morning, he responded. The rest is really history...we never looked back and only moved forward. Thank God for that.

If you haven't found your person yet, put a little star next to this because these kinds of partners are hard to find. Throughout the on-and-off again moments in our decade-long dating story, Eric never stopped being there for me in the moments that mattered most. He loves very similarly to his mama: unconditionally. And he believes in me—always has.

Was Eric perfect? Absolutely freaking not. Just like me, he was far from it. Regardless of where either of us was falling or failing, if I needed Eric, he was always there. And as we got older and life got heavier, he never wavered from picking up the pieces of me when I didn't have the capacity to lift myself. He's the greatest friend (and now partner) I could have ever asked for.

Eric tests me, pushes my buttons, drives me nuts, teases me more than I'd like, and refuses to acknowledge the fact that I'm actually funny. ☺

So after **twelve** years of the craziest roller coaster ride, Eric asked me to be his wife.

Just like everything else in our relationship, that didn't come without its obstacles or my sass. The six months leading up to our engagement, I was relentless...like what the heck is this man waiting for?!

We'd been back together for two years and were living together in St. Louis. We had finally found our grown-up rhythm. We were happy and having the time of our life. What was the hold up?!

In true Cassy fashion, I did not shy away from my feelings and made it **very** known that I was beyond over waiting. When his brother proposed to my sister-in-law, I all but had a stroke and received that news about as well as a flamingo being told it wasn't pink. It wasn't that I wasn't happy for them; I was just very unhappy for me...what a jerk (I was). I'm human too, y'all, for the good and the bad.

So on May 5, 2018, Eric and I were in an Uber on our way to my aunt and uncle's for a Cinco de Mayo party. Eric had been acting weird all morning, but I didn't think twice; it was going to be a great day.

As we headed downtown, our driver was going on and on about his upcoming wedding...poor Eric. Y'all know what's worse than hungry me? Bitter me.

I don't personally recall the level of theatrics, **but** Eric will share that I basically said we would never get married because we were going to be stuck dating forever. Again, poor Eric.

Little did I know, my engagement ring was sitting in Eric's pocket, and I was just minutes away from my *surprise* engagement party. Honestly though, if I were him, I would've been having second thoughts.

Shortly after arriving, we were standing on the rooftop patio and I'm just talking away about this Uber ride.

Talking, talking, talking.

Meanwhile, my friends and family are all hiding in a small bathroom inside. Eric finally interrupts me to ask for a picture with "downtown as the background" and he gets down on one knee.

Despite dreaming of this moment for over a decade and all but planning it myself (in my head), I regret to inform you that the first words out of my mouth were, "Shut up." Because apparently, in a state of absolute shock, I no longer had the ability to find real words. I could not believe it. It was and still is the best "yes," I ever made.

That day started a season of celebration that was and always will be some of the best moments of my life. We spent the weekend watching the Cubs with Eric's family and if that wasn't a full circle moment, I'm not sure what is. I was finally becoming a Williamson.

I didn't want a long engagement. The entire wedding had really been planned for years. I knew what I wanted, how I wanted it, and who I wanted at it. I just needed to find the place and the people to bring that vision to life.

After five months, I got to walk down the aisle to my very best friend. I still get teary-eyed thinking about that day and our vows to each other. That season is one I wish I could replay again and again; it would never get old.

Eric and I will never pretend to be something we aren't. We will never deny our history—the good, the bad, and the ugly. But one thing we continue to do is choose one another, fight for each other, love another, and support the other's dreams.

Unapologetic Truth #19: The People You Keep

Just like any other kind of relationship, marriage takes work. I share this short version (I promise) of our story with you in hopes that it will inspire you to always chase after the people who allow you to be Unapologetic.

I continue to mention the importance of the people around us as supporters, facilitators, and believers in our journey of growth. Eric has been the pillar, the lighthouse, and the foundation that I stand on. As I said in my vows, he's the best gift I've ever been given.

Eric challenges me, loves me, and believes in me with so much fierceness I don't have room to doubt myself when he's in the discussion. He's my toughest accountability partner. He pushed me to seek counseling, helped me with my homework, and stood by me as I've set some strong boundaries with people in my life.

Eric supports me in every crazy moment. He shows me grace, poise, and patience that I don't always deserve. He recognizes my weaknesses and handles them with kid gloves. He meets me where I am, loves me through the highs and the lows, and never tries to hold me back. He's all in, all the time, with all my big dreams.

I couldn't put into words how much I love him.

So I'll say it once more—but do not stop fighting for these people. If you have them, hold onto them. If you haven't found them, don't stop looking. Recognize the angels among you. Mine just happens to be my husband.

Whether it's a partner, parent, friend, family member, or coach, it doesn't matter what their title is, they will change your life.

• • •

Chapter Twenty

The Plunge into Parenthood

• • •

I went back and forth about including this chapter in the book, but I decided to leave it because much like the rest of my story, if it can resonate with just one person who needed to hear it, it's done its job. So let's dive right in...

I DID NOT CALL THIS SECTION the "plunge" into parenthood without good reason. If you're a parent, you know that becoming a first-time mom or dad feels like a plunge you never had enough time to get ready for, even if you thought you did.

We read the books, took the classes, had the certifications and went in feeling confident—but let me just say, you can prepare all you want, and for a lot of us, parenthood just isn't easy. It's not easy for **you** or for your marriage. Not to say it isn't for some people, y'all are the real MVPs, but for many of us, it's like whiplash, every day.

I'm going to reflect on my postpartum journey and transition back to work in the next chapter.

What I want to talk about in this chapter is how freaking hard the plunge into parenthood was on our marriage. I just got done telling you how, in my eyes, Eric all but hung the moon, so ask me why after we had our daughter I was genuinely concerned I might be headed for a feature on a future episode of *Snapped*?!

Something about bringing a human into the world just changes you. Forever. We're told that. But after having her, there weren't enough friends, baby gadgets, sweet baby snuggles, or deep breathing exercises to adequately prepare me for how during this time, something about Eric made him the most frustrating person on the planet.

Maybe it was just me. Maybe it was because it was half his fault. But the fact that I was a walking cow in recovery, leaking from all but a few openings of my body, while also simultaneously losing my hair (and sanity) tore me up from the outside in.

We were so prepared for our daughter and she was taken care of like a precious little celebrity on a private jet, but Eric and I...we were not prepared for the strain this would put on our relationship.

I was irritable, angry, resentful, happy, frustrated, excited, sad, weepy, surprised, tired, restless. You name it, I felt it.

For a bit of context, I was also counting my days and time by the number of Hallmark Christmas movies I watched. This phase did not serve me well.

Eric was working in medical device sales at the time and was actually being paged into the or during my delivery. Fortunately, he was able to decline that specific procedure, but he didn't have any paternity leave or time off, which honestly may have been what pushed us (me) over the edge.

While he got to go to work (see how I said that), I was a mom-machine responsible for milk supply, diaper changes, bottle cleaning, laundry management, and baby survival.

It was like the *Groundhog Day* Christmas Special.

My maternity leave did a number on me and being alone all day with our daughter was not easy. Of course I loved being with her, smelling her, watching her, and cherishing every second of those newborn snuggles. But I also felt isolated, unproductive, stressed, and bored.

I exclusively pumped, which meant that we bottle fed our daughter. This was a great system until it wasn't. Specifically, we were just fine until she and I were alone and had the unfortunate timing of her needing a bottle while I was pumping. This is when it could get complicated.

I will never forget having her do tummy time while I was pumping when she went from 0 to one-hangry (like 100 but worse). I was using my plug-in pump at the time, which basically meant I was connected to a cord while I also had two bottles attached to me like a cow hooked up to the automatic milking system. I was ready for business, but not going anywhere fast.

I "paused" to make a bottle, but here was the tricky part: Feeding her while finishing my pumping session.

Now, before you get all logical on me, let's just take a quick second to recognize that sleep deprivation means you're also oftentimes deprived of any sort of logical problem-solving skills. So instead of just taking the pump off, I was trying to pump and feed her. That was my first mistake.

This did not end well…I was crying, she was crying, milk was everywhere, and the Hallmark Christmas movie of that hour was rolling in the background. And then she projectile vomited everywhere on everything. It was like an SNL skit except I was actually living it, and no one was laughing. How could it be this hard?

These moments of absolute insanity just wrecked me. Where some likely stayed cool, calm, and collected, I felt like I was losing my mind.

I recognize this is not everyone's story. I'm fully aware that I suffered from postpartum in ways that others do not. But damn, I wish someone would've warned me about the potential of the "dislike your spouse" phase because as y'all know, this is my favorite person in the world and not liking him during one of the most challenging seasons of my life absolutely sucked.

I remember sitting on the couch crying to him and his parents about not feeling like myself. I was struggling with all of the things and feeling more alone than I ever had before. My in-laws hadn't had this experience and although they supported me, it was hard to feel like anyone could relate or understand what I was going through.

In case you haven't been there, this really just pushed me even further down the rabbit hole.

Eric met me with grace, patience, and love because that's who he is, but I didn't make it easy on us. What's more bizarre to me is that now, as I try, I can't even remember specific examples to share with you.

I remember talks with friends, vent sessions, and nights crying myself to sleep, but it goes to show that it's never as bad as it actually feels or seems in that moment. That or I've just blocked it out. Depression at its finest.

My solution was to start counseling again, exercise as I was able, and ease into work to give myself things that felt productive. Slowly, but surely, over time I started to find myself, my happy, and my love for my life and marriage again, but it wasn't without effort, self-awareness, and accountability from the people around me.

If you're a new mama finding yourself in a situation like mine, I'm praying you've found relief in knowing that you're not alone.

I didn't want to share this. It's hard for me to admit that this happened to me, but if it can help you at all—it's worth my vulnerability. Pay that forward to the people in your circle about to enter into a similar chapter.

It takes a village. You don't have to suffer through this season feeling alone. Chances are that your spouse, your family, your friends are all doing what they feel like they can do to help you. But only <u>you</u> can find solutions that work for **you**.

If you're having similar feelings, be proactive, communicate openly, ask for accountability, and fight for the human that was by your side before this AND will be by you on the other side of it.

Unapologetic Truth #20: Unapologetically Parenting

I was kicking butt and taking names in my journey to becoming Unapologetically Me before having my daughter. I was in a great place mentally, physically, and emotionally. Eric and my relationship had never been stronger. I was humbled when I became a mom and this all shifted. It took a lot of work, awareness, and asking for help to get myself back to baseline.

We all have to recognize that becoming a parent looks extremely different for everyone. Unfortunately, the world we're in also makes it a lot harder on us. The pressures that are placed on us through our society and social media only make these obstacles more challenging.

We can really lose ourselves playing the comparison game in a sea of photos, videos, and reels, but don't. People only share what they want to be seen. Focus on you, your relationship, and your little family. Y'all are so worth it.

Similarly to ignoring the noise of social media, don't get too caught up in the noise of the people around you either. I know our families mean well, but my goodness, everyone seems to have an opinion and man, they know their opinion is the "right" one.

The only solution here is to set clear boundaries and have open communication. Don't let anyone make you feel "less than" the parent you are.

In the midst of the madness, while you're riding the emotional roller coaster, please don't forget to take time to laugh.

It's so easy to get swept up and weighed down with everything that feels challenging. I found myself getting stuck worrying about doing things "by the book" or how I thought it had to be done that I would forget to enjoy what was happening right in front of me.

There are so many moments that we can find joy in when we let ourselves. We all know how funny a baby blowout can be. Nothing like finding yourself in a shitty situation with such a cute little human. ☺

Plunges are not meant to be easy, but I promise you light on the other side. The key for all of us newbie parents is to be willing, motivated, and ready to look for it.

And just remember, if you can't be Unapologetically You, how can you expect that sweet baby to grow up and be?

You're doing a great job and you're very much worth the work.

• • •

Chapter Twenty-One

Pouring Myself a Cup of Ambition

• • •

FOR AS LONG AS I CAN REMEMBER, I've been a high achiever. In case it isn't obvious, I have a strong drive, a type A personality, and prefer to be in control. During my last semester of graduate school, I was fortunate enough to be offered a position at the children's hospital where I was wrapping up my last clinical rotation.

Despite not graduating until May, I had accepted my first job as a speech-language pathologist (SLP) there in March. I was elated. I'd been working on this degree and for this job for seven years.

Although this would be my first "big girl gig," it felt like I'd been working my whole life. I started working as a babysitter at 11 for my neighbors, held a job with a worker's permit at 14, and continued work throughout high school and undergrad.

I even paid my way through graduate school despite being told by the program director that "students can't work while in the program." As some of you are aware, not all of us have a choice and I made it work, literally. It was never easy, but I graduated with a 3.9 GPA and a job offer.

Let people tell you that you can't do something, that's oftentimes when we do our best "doing."

Despite feeling prepared, educated, and trained for my first SLP job, there was a great deal of "trial by fire" working in a pediatric children's hospital. I was surrounded by fantastic clinicians who were more than willing to help guide me, teach me, and answer whatever crazy question I had that day. But I was determined to learn as quickly as possible.

I continued to study after hours. I poured into my patients when I was there and I worried about a lot of them when I went home. Working in the hospital was heavy and I still admire my friends who show up every day for those patients and their families. Not all superheroes wear capes.

In the fall of 2019, Eric and I made a big decision to move to Alabama to be closer to my family. We had no idea that the world was going to turn upside down six months later. I transitioned to a private practice and was hopeful that this would be "lighter" than what I was taking home with me from the hospital.

I had a caseload of 40+ kids averaging 14 sessions a day. This was my attempt to sustain the same income I had in St. Louis, and I was busting my butt to do it. It was at this clinic that I was gifted two of my most favorite humans. Looking back, and similar to graduate school, they are both most definitely the "why" for my time there.

My patients ranged from 18 months to 68 years old. I served individuals with speech, language, fluency, and/or cognitive disorders. However, the majority of my caseload was kiddos on the autism spectrum. I loved my kids. I loved getting to be a light in their day, see them flourish, and empower their families with the knowledge and skills that allowed them to communicate with their children. It was an absolute gift and there will always be a very special place in my heart for SLPs.

Therapy services took a very drastic and unplanned turn when the pandemic hit. I went from being able to provide exemplary services to being forced to implement virtual sessions. My one and only regret during that time is not recording myself during my attempts to not only engage but finagle a 2-year-old to work through a screen.

Those stories could write a book of their own—I really missed the boat on that one.

From the ridiculous, comedic attempts I made to get (and keep) their attention to the bizarre events I witnessed on the other side of the screen—I felt like a wannabe online magician (is there such a thing?) trying to do tricks just so my littles would participate.

Picture me **leaping** and I mean leaping out of my chair to make them laugh. That was just the tip of the iceberg. I made up games, mailed them surprises, and dressed up. We did whatever it took, and I know I was one of the many clinicians in this boat.

The very best part of all of this was that I never knew what would greet me when that patient link was opened on the other side. Y'all know the TV show *Love Is Blind*? It was like that but "speech therapy" edition.

I had sessions in the backseat of a moving car, in their parent's bed, or in the tiny hands of a six-year-old, which basically felt like riding a roller coaster.

Worst of all and for whatever bizarre reason, clothing somehow became optional for my patients during my sessions. I'm not kidding. It was wild and I was tired. Most days I felt defeated and ineffective, which was a hard place to be.

When we finally got back in-office, things were still weird, but everybody at least had clothes on, so for that I'm grateful. We had mask protocols in place and for a long time, I bent the rules with my littles.

It's impossible to do effective treatment for a non-verbal kiddo when your mouth is covered. I was fortunate that I had that ability. My friends working in the hospitals did not. Again, not all superheroes wear capes.

My God-wink here came while searching for a new home. Eric had found a lot that we both loved and we began shopping the idea of building a new home. We were sitting at the design center when the salesperson was asking us about what we do for work.

His mom was also a speech therapist. It was at that point when he asked me if I was looking for a job because he thought I could be really good at "this." I never say no to an interview, still don't, so I met with leadership.

The job they had at that time wasn't an appropriate fit for me and I still appreciate the owner recognizing that. I have a lot of drive, get bored easily, and need to be challenged. I want to believe he saw that. I chalked it up as "not meant to be." But, God had another plan.

It was March 11, 2021, and I was sicker than a dog. I felt like trash and couldn't stop throwing up. The problem was if I didn't go to work, I didn't get paid. I also had a full day of kids I needed to see. Naturally, being the stubborn human that I am, I had my sister drive me to work because I'd be fine. I was not fine.

After she had to escort me in, we both agreed that I needed to take my happy butt home and call it. So I did.

It was also at home that I took three pregnancy tests and discovered I didn't have the flu. I was pregnant. Believe it or not, that same day, I got a call from the owner whom I'd interviewed with a couple months prior offering me a job.

I took this as my sign that it was time to make a change and take a leap. If not for me, but for my future little family. I never thought after seven years of chasing my CCC's I'd leave the field, but I also knew that I could not be the mom I wanted to be in the position I was in. I was burned out and leaving most everything I had at that clinic every day.

I gave two months' notice in hopes that my kids would be taken care of. I remained sick almost every day and thank goodness I had the sweetest friends (for so many reasons).

Leaving two of my dearest colleagues turned friends, along with my kids, was absolutely brutal. During my exit, I cried most days with at least one of my families as I shared the news of my leaving. It was one of the hardest decisions I've ever had to make.

I was choosing myself and feeling extremely selfish in doing so, but I was also choosing my growing family, and I won't hold onto shame in that, ever.

In May of 2021, I started my new role as an online sales counselor and designer. The role was hybrid and allowed me to work both remotely and at the model home. I was quickly thrown into the deep end in an industry I knew nothing about.

I also had to tell my brand-new boss that I was pregnant. I was terrified. There was plenty stacked against me. I was brand new to the role with no experience and could not afford to lose my job. I hustled twice as hard my entire pregnancy and was thankful that shortly after my first trimester I finally stopped puking.

Similar to previous experiences, I was immersed in a circle of amazing humans. From designers, lenders, surveyors, trades, and wonderful co-workers, I was surrounded by people who believed in me, poured into me, wanted to see me succeed, and vice versa.

I loved each of them as hard as I could and am still so grateful. Fortunately, I'm still able to love on so many of them. They're relationships I'll cherish forever.

Unapologetic Truth #21: An Ode to Dolly

As I've transitioned from music to healthcare to new home sales and the building industry, I've recognized a very consistent pattern.

No matter the industry, regardless of my position, and despite how long I'd been with an organization, with each and every place, there have been people and lessons that have served my life in very big ways.

Whether they were good or bad is less relevant and shouldn't be your focus.

What I want you to consider is that regardless of where you're thriving in a job or feeling stuck, there's a reason that you're there.

Whether it's a person, a skill, an obstacle, or an innovation, there's always something to learn from the places we find ourselves. I've personally walked away with at least one thing that served my bigger purpose with each experience.

Keep in mind, it often wasn't until I was reflecting back on my time that I was able to realize how deeply something or someone served me. I would consider the same in your own professional life.

Are you happy where you are? Asking yourself the following questions can help uncover whether your current path is aligned with your purpose.

If yes:

- What about the experience is serving you?
- What about it is challenging you?
- Who is impacting your life positively?
- Whose life are you impacting?

If no:

- What about the position is making you unhappy?
- Do you enjoy the work?
- Do you enjoy the people?
- Do you enjoy the culture?

Depending on those answers above, where is the breakdown?

If you answered "no" to the above questions, please know that you can't stay where you aren't being served and you can't grow where you aren't able to serve the people or the space around you.

If you're unhappy, you've gone stagnant, or if you feel like you're living the same day on repeat, what's your stuck for staying exactly where you are?

What can you do to challenge yourself?

What needs to happen for you to fill up that cup of ambition again?

Most of us started with it at one point, so how do you elicit that again?

Remember, if you aren't uncomfortable, you're not growing. If you're not growing, you're likely not moving toward your bigger purpose. This all leads you to the road of being Unapologetic.

My drive has been propelling me forward for as long as I can remember. But both my passion and growth have been largely impacted by the adversity, experiences, and people I've met along the way.

I would not be who I am or where I am today if it hadn't been for the experiences that led me here, good and bad. The key to learning from an experience and growing from it is being intentional about your reflection on what each taught you.

If you haven't taken the time to do this for yourself, this is the perfect place to start.

• • •

Chapter Twenty-Two

A Salute to Working Mamas

• • •

WHETHER YOU'RE A WORKING MOM, stay-at-home mom, dog mom, cat mom, or have a pet gerbil...there's truly a lesson or two in here for all of us. But, I'd be lying to myself and you if I didn't explain how humbling it has been for me to be a working mom to a baby and now a toddler.

Before becoming a mama, I'd been very busy building my career. I also made a drastic, dramatic, and extreme career change within my first few months of my pregnancy. In true Cassy fashion, I went all in despite my "condition" and planned on managing everything accordingly for my maternity leave (or so I thought).

Just a few weeks before my due date, our one and only salesperson put in her two-week notice. This really threw a wrench in the plan as she was intended to be my coverage while I was out. I couldn't help but feel that I was leaving my entire team out to dry without anyone to support the sales team, so I didn't.

I'm not proud to admit that while sitting in the hospital bed between my sleeping newborn and husband, I was emailing a customer about her contract. They signed that evening but only after that correspondence from me.

This is not a "woohoo" moment or even worthy of a celebration. It is most definitely **not** an example I want to set for anyone. **And** they turned out to be one of the most challenging customers of my career. I share that because nothing and no one is worth sacrificing your family for.

Throughout what was supposed to be my maternity leave, I took customer calls, managed contracts from afar, communicated with the team, and even went as far as completing a virtual design appointment from my house in an effort to keep up with as much as I could. This was all while managing a newborn and postpartum.

10/10 **Do not** recommend.

I'll admit the behavior was partially because I'm a workaholic and partially because I knew my team didn't have anyone else. I couldn't be the reason we didn't have anything to build in the next couple of months just because I decided to have a baby. We were already a small team, and my leave put us a man down.

With that being said…

If I could turn back the clock, I would tell myself to turn it off. Put the phone down. Walk away. Leave it alone. But you know what we can't do?

Turn back time.

> If you're an expecting mama or a new mom, that precious newborn time is something you can never get back. It is chaotic, sweet, brutal, wonderful, and so short all at the same time. You blink and it's over.

But the craziest part for me was that no one was really making me work. Sure, I was getting calls and emails, but I was making an erratic choice based upon this toxic belief that I was failing if I didn't respond, act, or work.

I have a strong drive, a type A personality, and a lot of control issues, remember?

I so regret sacrificing that time with my daughter for a JOB. That's all it is, y'all. It's a job.

And you know where we will always be replaceable? At work.

Can you guess the one place where we are irreplaceable? I don't have to tell you.

This is why I have to salute working mamas because when you become a mom and go back to work, you're faced with this balancing act every. single. day.

The mom guilt was real (still is), but the guilt I felt about not working was also crippling. I had no idea how much of my identity was tied to my work until I couldn't work. I mean, I'd been doing it my entire life. I wasn't about to slow down now.

It was at this point when I really started to "fail." Failure in my eyes meant dropping the ball, forgetting things, completing a task at half the capacity I would've prior.

Was I actually failing? No. Did it feel like I was? Absolutely. Cue my postpartum anxiety and depression.

This version of me ranks right up there with sixth grade Cassy and graduate school Cassy in my hall of shame book for myself. Not a version of myself I'm proud of.

The problem was, just like those times before, I wasn't myself. But this time, I knew it and I had an extreme emotional response to her. I hated this version of me.

I was a mad, moody, unstable wreck. I was absolutely lost. I was defeated, frustrated, and let down. I couldn't believe that "this" was my new reality. So I got myself right back into counseling because I was not about to let myself spiral. It wasn't even about me anymore either. I was now responsible for the most precious, beautiful life and I had to fight for not just myself, but her too.

A month after coming back from maternity leave and after only 10 months of being with the company, I was moved into the Director of Sales and Marketing position. Remember our beautiful discussion about how failure is just learning the hard way? Wish I could've read that chapter to myself during this season. As a new mom and new leader, I felt like I was failing someone or something every moment of every day. Key words: "felt like." Was I actually? No, but this was crippling.

Seeing that I don't like losing or failing the people around me, my anxiety skyrocketed, and I felt completely out of control of my own life.

I will never forget the day I drove my four-month-old to our model home for a design appointment. Our childcare fell through, and I had no option not to take her. It was about a 45-minute drive to the model, and I gave us both quite the pep talk.

We got there without an issue and had a great day overall. She got so much love from the team, and everyone chipped in with helping. But as the day went on, I knew my lucky clock was ticking and I needed to get us home. As soon as we got in the car, she completely came apart and became inconsolable despite my attempts to calm her down from the front seat.

I couldn't figure out what was wrong with her and after a few minutes of nonstop hysteria, I pulled over into a gas station parking lot. I knew my options were slim, especially before we had to get on the interstate. So there we went.

In the midst of her screaming bloody murder, me taking her out of her car seat, and also feeling like I personally was about to implode, her Wubba (pacifier) fell out onto the black asphalt. Mind you, we're in a not-at-all-clean gas station parking lot. I didn't even have a chance to notice because I was too panicked thinking about how the hell I was going to get us both home.

It was around this time that a mom of two older kids came running up to the car shouting at me. As she got closer, I was able to make out that she had noticed the pacifier falling and was picking it up off the ground for me, frantically doing her best job to clean it.

Y'all, you know how they say moms just know? This woman must have just seen it on my face because she looked at me with the kindest smile and said, "You're doing a great job, Mom. It's going to get easier." Bless this stranger and saint of a human.

If I hadn't both been absolutely hysterical right alongside my screaming baby, I would've taken the time to hug this woman and tell her how much she meant to me in that moment. Unfortunately, all I could do was blubber out a pitiful "thank you" and get myself and my daughter back in the car.

This mama was right though; it was going to get easier. But it'd be another year before I'd really feel like myself again and recognize that. All the more reason we mamas have to stick together. This random act of kindness meant more to me than she could ever know. God-winks.

Looking back now, I think it's essential we recognize our triggers. If we can't in the moment, then we should at least work to identify them after the fact to be proactive in the future. I'm not sure about any other mamas reading this, but the straw that broke this camel's back was pumping. I know that now.

At the time, the country was in the middle of a formula shortage so as a "producer," I felt like I had no other option but to keep pumping (even though I absolutely hated it). I felt so much guilt for even considering formula, considering there were families out there who didn't have a choice, along with very scarce resources available. So I continued with the torture.

But no one could've ever prepared me for the mockery I'd face while pumping at work. It was an HR nightmare. Despite what I'm sure most of my colleagues meant as jokes, they got old really quick. While pumping, I was called "robo-boobs" or "robo-Dolly."

The men on my team would mock and act out the sound of my hands-free pump any time they could. And last, but certainly not least, it was frequently verbalized what an inconvenience I was to the team when I had to take an extra break or interrupt a meeting to remove my pumps and store everything.

I would call Eric from the bathroom sobbing about how hard it was, but without the option for formula, I didn't know what to do. After five months, I completely crumbled. I gave it up completely because the stress of having to manage it alongside work was making everything 10x worse.

I look back and still can't believe that's how I was treated. I'm sure the team would say it was a joke or that I needed to get thicker skin, but for anyone dealing with postpartum, you and I both know that "thick skin" is so far out of our reach.

I had been in the Director of Sales and Marketing role for about four months when I was selected to speak in front of 500 sales leaders sharing my best practice for a Sales Leadership Summit in Austin, Texas. It was after coming off that stage that I first told the founder I wanted a job. I continued to tell him for 14 months. It was in late September of 2023 that I had an offer to work as their Chief Evangelist and Brand Ambassador. I was announcing my new role the same week my baby girl turned two.

This next chapter would present a new set of challenges to me, my family, and my marriage. But just like every opportunity before this one, it would teach me some life-changing lessons while introducing me to some of my now greatest friends.

Unapologetic Truth #22: More than Enough

No matter what title you hold, what job you have, or where you are in your journey, it will always be an uphill battle to be the best mom, the best wife, the best friend, the best daughter, the best _____ and the best employee.

It's honestly too much.

The pressure we continue to put on ourselves is also extremely damaging.

Women are not machines. We are people.

During this transition, I felt alone, isolated, depressed, and so guilty. At times, I still deal with these feelings. But I haven't let life beat me yet and I certainly wasn't going to then or now. My saint-like counselor challenged my own narrative, the conversations I was having with myself, and my "whys" on several occasions on this journey to my new normal. I've learned a lot about grace, mindfulness, and self-talk during this transition into motherhood and I hope in sharing this with you, you feel less alone too.

I continue to struggle my way through finding balance and boundaries. I refuse to sacrifice the big dreams I have for myself while also raising a family. I've seen far too many women not only do it but absolutely crush it. We are capable and we are worthy.

What I've come to realize is that much like so many of the other lessons we've already discussed together, it goes back to grace.

New mamas, old mamas, working mamas, stay-at-home mamas, we need a lot of grace (and Jesus). Although I think most of us are great at giving it, showing it, and even are fortunate enough to have people around us sharing it with us, I think the biggest obstacle we have to overcome is to give that same grace to ourselves. We have to give ourselves grace.

Similar to what I wish I could've told my 11-year-old self, we're never as alone as we feel. In moments of adversity, we can't forget how far we've come. We have more power than we could ever imagine.

And for the mamas who are in a different season, recognize the power you have to pay grace and kindness forward. Be like the mom who stopped what she was doing to help and lift me up in the parking lot that day. I've said it once, I've said it twice, and I'll say it again, it takes a village.

Chapter Twenty-Three

Pick a Seat at the Right Table

• • •

DO Y'ALL REMEMBER your lunch hour at school growing up?

Pick a movie set in a school and picture their depiction of the school cafeteria. I always think of *Can't Buy Me Love* with Patrick Dempsey. I swear half of that movie was happening in the courtyard during their lunch.

I think all of us recall the shape, form, color, and/or smell of the food that was served, I'm looking at you, rectangle pizza. But really I want to reminisce for a bit about the social aspect of lunch.

Where did you sit?

In grade school, I remember being assigned a table with my class, but you picked your seat. In middle school, it depended on the school. And in high school, anything was fair game, sit where you want, until the next bell.

No matter the school, or the grade—one thing was consistent, the table you picked and the seat you sat in was pretty much your spot for the year. You had your group and your group, had their spot. Rarely did you see people move around. And as far as the Hollywood filmmakers are concerned, your spot in the cafeteria dictated your place on the social ladder.

It was a decision that stuck with you for the year.

But what happened if during the year a relationship changed?

What did you do if there was a fall out among friends?

How did we navigate, as kids, the social experiment that was (and probably still is) the school cafeteria?

I ask these questions, because I think it's an extremely interesting concept that translates into a deeper lesson as we grow older. As kids, we made lighthearted decisions about friendships, spots at a certain table, or maybe even seats on the bus.

I don't remember making these decisions with a great deal of strategy in mind, but maybe you did. Either way, I have to ask how we end up making similar decisions as adults?

How do we know what table to sit at?

How do we know if we've picked the right seat?

Let the table be your friends, your job, or your desired degree and let the seat represent your spot, role, or position.

Although my experiences have been primarily through a great deal of trial and error—I've learned more than a few lessons along the way.

Regardless of where you are in your journey, it's imperative that you set a high standard for both the table you choose to place yourself and your seat at that table. I also want to caution you that showing up Unapologetic will oftentimes mean:

- If there isn't a spot at the table, you have to be willing to make one
- If you find yourself at a table without a seat that serves you, be willing to walk away and find another table
- Despite any hardships, you won't apologize for who you are and the value you bring

Let's unpack each of these a bit.

If there isn't a spot at the table, you have to be willing to make one

Have you ever been in a situation where you weren't sure where you fit? Or maybe there hasn't been anyone quite like you there before? Do you see the seat for you there?

If you answered "yes," to these questions, this is your opportunity to be a catalyst. More specifically, you have to be open to the idea that it may be up to you to create a seat at the right table.

Picture yourself finding those two friends you **love** in the cafeteria and squeezing yourself between them, wiggling elbows and all, barely resting on that space between benches because you want to be there with them that bad.

The same idea applies here.

You've found the place you want to be, you know you're at the right table, but you have to find your spot.

This could look like creating a new position, advocating for someone like you in an already established position, or innovating the role you're currently in. No matter which of these applies, I'd challenge you to be open to the idea that sometimes only **we** can make room for ourselves at the right table.

You have to be willing to write your own job description, pitch exactly "why" you make the right person for the job, and/or get creative on how you can advance an opportunity for yourself with the current organizational structure.

Don't be afraid to blaze your own trail.

If you find yourself at a table without a seat that serves you, be willing to find another table

Are you familiar with the phrase, "Round peg in a square hole"? If not, it's the concept of not fitting in a particular space or situation. I cannot tell you how many times I've personally been a round peg trying to fit myself into a square hole.

Although, it's undoubtedly happened to all of us. We've been in places with friends, family, or at work where we've shrunk ourselves to fit in. Whether it's not answering a question we knew the answer to, holding back from making a comment, or contributing in agreement to something we actually didn't agree with at all.

Why do we do this?

I think it's for the same reason we did it in the school cafeteria. We want to keep our seat at the table. We don't want to be a disruptor. We want to be liked and we like to stay "safe."

But I'm here to say that I think all of us could benefit from a bit more disruption. I think we could all afford a few seized opportunities to speak up, stand up, or show up in ways that we feel called.

If you're at the right table, this will serve you in the greatest of ways. But you also have to recognize that at the wrong table, your peers won't be as receptive. Brace yourself for this. It's okay to accept that if the table no longer serves you, you may have to find another one.

You cannot embrace being Unapologetic if you're at the wrong table.

You won't apologize for who you are and the value you bring

I can't tell you the amount of calls I've had with the disruptors in different industries who've been undervalued, undermined, and underutilized because of the different energy, perspective, and insight they bring to the table.

In reading that, you might be thinking that energy, perspective, and insight, especially in the right places, should be celebrated. I agree with you. However, in many organizations, this is just not the case. Instead, they feel forced to compromise their voice to keep a title, position, or seat at the table.

Unapologetic Truth #23: Born to Stand Out

If there's one thing I know to be true in **any** relationship, including work, it's that you should not have to change who you are to "fit." Instead, you have to be willing to search for the people, places, and organizations that fit you. Round peg, round hole.

> I believe there is somewhere for everyone just like there is someone for everyone, should you seek it.

Recognize that in being Unapologetic, you're aligning yourself with people, culture, vision, core values, and growth that all serve your bigger purpose.

Now, is this my way of saying stick it to "the man"? No—not necessarily. What I'm saying is that you should never compromise yourself for a seat at the table.

Don't lose sight of what makes you so perfectly **you** in your journey to success.

• • •

Chapter Twenty-Four

Make A Difference: Servant Leadership

• • •

WHEN I WAS IN HIGH SCHOOL, I wrote a song called "Make a Difference." This song, which I consider my life's anthem, was inspired by personal experiences. Specifically, those with the people in my life who made a significant impact serving others. Each verse represents one of those people with the chorus focusing on their (and my) core values.

Mr. Lavin, a teacher.
My dad, a soldier.
Dr. Steh, my long-time pediatrician.

I shared a bit of the lyrics with you earlier in the book, but for the sake of this section, here's the chorus again:

> *"What do you do to make a difference?*
> *How will you sacrifice?*
> *Be a leader and a fighter.*
> *Make a difference, change a life."*

These words were not only lyrics, but a reminder that no matter who we are, where we're from, how old we are, what we do, or how much money we make, every single one of us has the power to Make a Difference. Similar to what I shared about the Angels Among Us.

Far too many people don't realize how much good a single person can actually do. How much **you** can actually do. We're crippled by an excuse like the list I shared above or lack the confidence to believe in our own power.

I'm a frequent flier at our local Dunkin' Donuts. I won't tell you how many rewards points I have, that's irrelevant. But our local store opened when my daughter was maybe six months old and we've been going on regular Donut Dates ever since.

Throughout this time period, we've gotten to know the staff and they've watched her grow. She went from a baby eating a chocolate frosted donut to three-going-on-13 placing her own order. She still gets the frosted donut by the way, but she's a much more effective consumer now. Of course, the staff has had turnover, but a constant has been Ms. Pam and her family. Believe it or not, at one point, Pam, her daughter, AND her granddaughter all worked there together.

Pam and her granddaughter were easy to get to know. Their family was always friendly and happy to see us. They knew our faces, names, and orders, whether we were in the drive-thru or dining in. When they were there, the service was not only warm, but efficient. When they weren't there—let's just say, we missed them.

Pam got sick and was quickly hospitalized. During this period of time, she actually got fired and so did her daughter, as they had missed too much work. I was heartbroken as I only knew of this news through a Facebook post from her granddaughter. I was baffled with this decision and couldn't understand where it came from. But, I figured we wouldn't see them again.

On my way to the airport one morning, I pulled up to the drive-thru and there was Pam! It'd been about a month since we'd seen her and I exclaimed, "Pam!" as I pulled up to the window.

I asked her, "What the heck happened?!"

Her response was poised and kind as she shared with me that once discharged from the hospital, she came and fought for her job back. She explained that at 62, it was hard to find work and she loved her job, she loved our community.

Cue the Love 'Em Down Cassy moment.

I went on to tell Pam how much we missed her. I shared with her what a light she was to our mornings and how grateful we were to see her back in action. I also went on to reference how darkness doesn't take from other darkness. She has a light to shine. What an example she was setting for her girls (two generations) about fighting for your light even when it's challenging and uncomfortable. She was truly rising above it and doing so with kindness, grace, and a smile on her face.

In this moment, with Pam in the drive-thru window and me in my car, her eyes welled up with tears. Her response of gratitude was overwhelming and made me emotional (major weeper).

You see, Pam had no idea the impact she'd made on my life and on my daughter's life. She was not aware of how much power her kindness, consistency, and friendliness meant to our morning Donut Dates. Why? Because the world hadn't told her so. Because when life beats us down, it's really easy to forget our impact. It doesn't matter who you are, where you are, or what you're doing, you have the power to create a positive impact on the people around you. And how freaking cool is that?

What an absolute gift we **get** to hold.

I'll say we should be loving on the Pams of the world a lot more than we do. We really need them. We need people like her spreading their light, goodness, and love. There's far too much negativity and it's easy to get caught up in the crap.

Since I couldn't hug Pam, I just reached out for her hand. I told her how much I appreciated her and how thankful I was to see her. I wished her a great day and just reminded her that life is far too short to let other people take away from the light we have to share with the world. We both agreed that was the truth! I drove off in tears, God-winks.

So at sixteen, this song was just the first step for me. It was the launching point. I was fortunate enough to sing it across the country with my sister and watch its message inspire individuals of all ages and walks of life.

As I've grown older, these lyrics have evolved into what has formed my passion for servant leadership.

No matter what job I have, no matter where I live, no matter what phase of life I've found myself in, there's always been a common denominator for me: service.

Now am I a picture-perfect postcard of service? Nope. I can get sassy and mess it up, just ask Eric. But I am grounded by this belief. I will find my way back to it no matter what darkness is thrown my way.

My decisions, actions, and passion have revolved around how I can pour into the people around me. I'm pretty sure I have a culmination of the love languages. I'm a unicorn when it comes to all of the different personality tests, including that one.

But since our time working with military kids, I've been driven by elevating others. I want to empower the people I come in contact with to believe in the very best version of themselves, feel more confident, recognize there are no limits to what they can achieve, and affirm that nothing can stop them from being exactly who they want to be, who they were called to be.

An important note here is this: I didn't wait until I was at an executive level to do any of this. Put a star here, highlight this, fold your page.

Do you know why this is so critical? Because you don't need a title to lead.

That's right, you don't need a title to lead. Whether you're the lowest person on the totem pole or the CEO of the company, you have the power to **lead**.

Leadership is a **choice**, not a *title*. It's the choice to put your focus, energy, and belief in the people around you. This is true for both work and our day-to-day life. Think of Pam.

In middle school, as a complete outcast, I felt called to serve and stand up for those struggling to find their voice.

In high school, still an outcast, my sister and I sought to support our military community through our journey with "The Price of Peace."

Professionally, I've succeeded through holding a place of leadership, but I've also made an impact throughout that time as an informal leader.

Some moments of *leadership* were big, and others were very small.

Some were at work, and some were in a drive-thru.

★ Leadership doesn't have to be a big, grand gesture. You can't perceive it as placing the flag on the moon. If you do, you won't ever be able to visualize it for yourself. I don't know many moon goers, do you?

We can't paint it to be unattainable. Instead, we have to see it exactly as it is in our own life.

For me, leadership is a lot of moving pieces. I believe it to be:

- Standing up for what's right, not just what's popular
- Helping the people around us
- Spreading light in even the darkest of circumstances
- Leaving the places or people around us a little better than you found them

Leadership is a conscious decision we continue to make, every single day. It's not a checked box, interview question, or a word after your email signature. Leadership is a living action.

Unapologetic Truth #24: Purpose over Perfection

Leadership is not a place that requires perfection. I know I've failed more times than I can count. I've made mistakes that I wish I could take back, I made decisions out of comfort, and I've let ego get in the way of my own growth. But through failure comes learning and through learning comes change.

The beauty of this is that there are no prerequisites to lead. All you need is a heart of servitude. The drive to make a positive impact. The hope to Make a Difference. So be bold in your attempts to lead, exactly where you are, right now. It will be worth it, I assure you.

And I will tell you; we need you. We really do. The world is desperate for strong leaders. We're immersed in a results-driven culture where we're forgetting the most important piece of the puzzle: our people.

Instead, we're oversaturated with micromanagers, disconnected executives, and emotionless bosses who've forgotten what should always be our driving force. Although these individuals oftentimes have the grit, knowledge, and vision, they lack the "people purpose." They fail to acknowledge, support, and fuel what their people crave the most. Do you know what that is? To be treated, seen, and valued as what we are...**people**.

It's not lost on me that this concept isn't rocket science. But my goodness, for some reason, thousands of organizations across the globe continue to ignore these simple truths. Organizations lack culture, integrity, and empathy. "A players" are flying off the shelf and fleeing what should be fantastic opportunities because of a lack of those three things.

So how do we change that? With you, of course.

One leader at a time.

It's up to us to show up, serve, and inspire. It's like the domino effect that only just needs a **lot** more pieces in the game.

I want you to ask yourself:

- What kind of leader are you?
- What can you do to make a difference?
- What can you do to change a life?

This desire to Make a Difference has always been my "mission" and always will be. My hope is that in my effort to Make a Difference, I can inspire you to do the same for the people around you. And for you to find a way to "hear" this *song* throughout all aspects of your life.

• • •

Chapter Twenty-Five

For My Girls

. . .

AS A PARENT, I think raising kids in the world we find ourselves in can be extremely challenging. And that's putting it lightly.

Before I even had my first daughter, I remember having some very raw and vulnerable conversations with my husband because I was scared. It felt uneasy to bring her into the world knowing what we know about it.

How do we protect our youth today?

How do we raise them "right" in the current climate we find ourselves in?

How do we model for them behaviors that will allow them to grow and be successful? Whatever that may look like for them as individuals.

Growing up for me was hard. I've shared that with you. I've lived a life of feeling like I didn't belong or fit even well into adulthood. So how do I as a mother prepare and equip my girls for any of it?

You can read parenting books, you can study behavior and psychology, and you can mend your own trauma as much as you're capable, but will it be enough?

How do we raise little humans to grow in a world that fights against being Unapologetic?

I wish I had a more straightforward answer for this, but I don't. Instead, I want to tell you about an astronaut, cowboy, firefighter, and princess I know very well who I think we can all draw inspiration from.

You see, my three-year-old loves dress-up. And although dress-up is really meant for playing at home, there have been moments where we've stretched the rules and let a magical, make-believe version of herself leave the house.

And when we have, do you know what I've seen happen?

The magic is magnified.

We were fighting with our daughter over a mermaid costume when Eric and I waved our white flag and said, we're not going. Our plans to go out to lunch were derailed by a very persistent three-year-old's desire to leave the house dressed as a mermaid. This particular ensemble was not appropriate for the weather or the place. So we threw up our hands and agreed to stay home. Everyone went on without us.

At the house, the game of make believe continued and this mermaid transformed into an astronaut. And not just any astronaut, but a royal one. Cue the "oohs" and "ahhs." So there before us was our daughter in her spacesuit, princess crown, and cowboy boots. She was beautiful in every way. She was also past the point of being overtired. Dress-up **IS** exhausting.

We decided to load her up, drive around, and let her sleep since, at this point, our child only naps when in the confines of a moving vehicle. Off we went.

To our surprise, she didn't fall asleep. So there we were in the Food City parking lot with a little astronaut whose hair was ready for the royal ball while her feet were ready for the rodeo. We had no choice but to take her in exactly as she was.

As we browsed each aisle, the same phenomenon kept happening.

Older kids saw her and smiled. Women complimented her attire and how beautiful she was. Men giggled at the sight. And the happiness that she prompted with her magical attire was contagious.

Fast forward to her annual check-up. This appointment happened to fall on the same day as "Dress Like Your Favorite Character" day at school. So, there we were again, walking into the doctor's office as Woody from *Toy Story*—cowboy hat and all.

Can you guess what happened? The same exact thing that happened in the grocery store. The magic was contagious. She was a walking facilitator of light, happiness, and joy.

Now, at three you get away with a lot more and I recognize that. But why? Is it because as our kids grow older, we push them further into the "box" of whatever the world says they're supposed to be?

I have to ask you, where do we lose the magic?

Because I don't believe our kids lose it on their own. I think the standards, expectations, and norms we place on them drive the magic out. What do you think?

My favorite part about this adventure to the doctor's office is how it ended.

Eric texted me after school dropoff to share that our daughter was the **only** one in her class who participated in dress-up. The other kids were wearing themed t-shirts, but no one else was in a full-on costume.

Here's the best part: She walked in, took no notice, sat down in her chair, and was eager to join her class just like any other day.

Do you want to know why I love this so much?

Because I want her to forever and always walk into a room, Unapologetically Herself, and not think twice. Just. Like. This.

> I want her confidence to be unshakable. I want her to feel comfortable in her own skin, exactly as she is. I want her to know and believe that she is MAGIC (because she is).

And when the world tells her she isn't, I hope and pray that she has so much of the above that it doesn't matter to her.

But y'all know where this starts? With us.

Unapologetic Truth #25: Boldly Beautiful

How can we raise confident humans if we aren't confident ourselves?

How can we expect them to not be dictated by social media or a life of comparison if we are?

How can our next generation feel good about the skin they're in when we don't?

It starts with you. And I know that's heavy, I know that's a lot of pressure, but you can do this. We can achieve it. If you can't embrace being Unapologetic for yourself alone, do it for them. Ever try to hold a determined parent back from their child?

One word: Run. You are unstoppable when it comes to your capabilities, especially as a parent. We cannot raise the next generation to reach their fullest potential, achieve their goals, and find their life's purpose if we aren't fostering an environment in which we are Unapologetically Ourselves.

So as we reflect on the work that needs to be done, if you're a parent reading this, consider how you can begin breathing these principles into your babies. It doesn't matter if they're young or old, toddlers or teens, it's never too late to start working toward living a big life. What a beautiful thing you could do alongside one another if they're old enough.

So where do you start?

• • •

Chapter Twenty-Six

Keep Shining

• • •

IF YOU DIDN'T KNOW IT, I'm so glad you're here. I'm grateful you've found your way to these pages.

You've learned more than a few things about me, my Cassy-isms, my crazy, and the adventures I've been on.

A Cassy-ism I use frequently that I want to share with you now is to Keep Shining. What this means for me is that we've all got a story, each of us has a past, and everyone carries some level of trauma around with them. That's life.

But what I think we forget is how bright each and every one of our lights are. A wise me once said, the sun can't do its job if it's not willing to let other people see it shine. This is true of you too…Remember Ms. Pam? The world needs us to *Keep Shining* and sometimes we just need that loving reminder.

This isn't an ask to walk around like a human ball of sunshine, that's definitely not for everyone. But it is meant to serve as your gentle nudge that you have a purpose that's big, beautiful, and great so keep shining. Or as Dory would say, "Just Keep Swimming."

My path to paving this way for myself can be defined in one word: boundaries.

As much as it has felt like I've poured every piece of my soul on these pages, I think it's important to note that I've chosen to "safeguard" a lot too.

I couldn't possibly share everything with you, and I wouldn't want to.

> One of the most important lessons I've learned through counseling is that for us to: grow, thrive, learn, evolve, impact, remain Unapologetically Ourselves, and keep shining we have to **protect our own peace**.

We have to protect our own peace. So as you move through the next steps in your journey to embracing the *Unapologetically You* that you were meant to be, I'd like to encourage you to set boundaries. That will look different for each of us, but I promise, we need them.

If you're not sure what this looks like, let's start simple.

The easiest way to practice this is with a situation where you're unsure you want to put yourself in. For the sake of practice, let's say you decide to go to a social event with people you don't like. You're in decision mode and you've got that gut feeling saying, "Ugh, I'm not sure I want to go because ____."

This is normally your God-wink to talk this out with yourself or an accountability partner.

Here are a few general questions to ask yourself when working through your next decision:

- Does saying "yes" to ____ serve me? (Side note: when we say "serve," this means it makes you feel good, aligns with your goals, helps you grow, and fills your bucket.)
- Does saying "yes" put my peace at risk?
- Is this the best use of my emotional, physical, or mental energy?
- How does doing ____ leave me feeling?

Mind you, these are simple, starting points to get you thinking about what places, people, and tasks fill your tank or take from it.

There's a fantastic children's book I reference called *Have You Filled a Bucket Today?* and it references the importance of being a "bucket filler" and not a "bucket dipper." It is truly as simple as it is. We want to fill and pour into others' lives, not take from them. Although this concept is fit for adolescents, the concept is really applicable to all age groups.

If something isn't serving us, and it's okay to be self-reflective here, we can't possibly live an Unapologetically, full, purpose-driven life.

If we continue to put ourselves in spaces that deplete what's in our bucket, we won't have anything left to give the world around us. It contradicts all the good that we're working toward. That's why it's so imperative we recognize what in our life is draining us both personally and professionally.

It's equally important to create a plan for accountabilities and hold true to them.

Why? Because life isn't and won't always be sunshine and rainbows. We won't always be in a bucket-filling space.

There are going to be people, things, and experiences that disappoint you. There will be moments that turn out different than you expected. You will face defeat, hardships, and frustration just like the rest of the world.

I challenge you to Keep Shining.

I've shared that I'm Functioning and Fighting. How many times is too many to say I'm not perfect? I'm a work in progress on this too, but I'm working on it. I hope you will too. I battle myself regularly and refuse to give up on her. I will continue to choose light over the darkness and when I fail, I will lean into those around me to remind me.

I will fight for my very best self every day so that the people I love and care about have exactly what they deserve, the very best version of me. I will Keep Shining so that others are hopefully inspired to do the same.

Why will you Keep Shining?

Who are you shining for?

Life is funny and will serve you with unexpected twists and turns. One chapter will always have to end for another one to begin. During these transitions, remember that no matter what chapter you find yourself in, you have a choice to shine, succeed, and Make a Difference.

Keep your head up and never stop fighting for the place you can shine the brightest. I'm cheering for you.

Conclusion

Big Hugs and Love

• • •

I HAVE TEARS streaming down my face as I write this closing chapter.

Oh, how badly I wish I could sit across from you like an excited friend as you read these final words.

But since I can't, please picture Agnes Gru on *Despicable Me* seeing the "fluffy unicorn" for the first time. If you haven't seen it, Google it because I tried to put it in the book but was rejected by people who love me and know copyright law.

If you chose to read this book because you're trying to find yourself, feeling stuck without direction, hoping to unlock your true potential, or all of the above, it's not something that you can do from reading this book alone.

It takes work.

Remember when I said it takes a village?

Having a tribe of people to lean into is essential in becoming Unapologetic.

These are the people who will inspire you, challenge you, educate you, pour into you, and support you. These beautiful humans will believe in you when you've lost your way or faith in yourself.

If you're missing your tribe like I was, don't lose hope.

Do you want to know how you find these people?

With Big Hugs and Love. [Maybe actually, maybe not.]

The important thing to note is that we cannot receive anything in life if we aren't open to it. Let me repeat that...We cannot get anything if we aren't OPEN to it.

So **get comfy with being uncomfy** and start asking for a seat at the table. If you're drawn to someone, go after them. If you want the job, ask for it. If you're feeling called to a place, find a way to get yourself there.

It's like what we tell our kids, you will never know if you don't try.

Can I share my crazy Cassy strategy with you?

I ask people out all the time. That's right, I do. I'm not ashamed. I set up coffee dates, happy hours, lunch dates, you name it! I'm proud to say I've got a pretty good track record for getting that first "yes."

Did they all work out? Absolutely not, YIKES…But just like a bad first date, when it **does** work out, gosh, aren't we always so glad that we did it?

If it's meant to be, it will be. If it isn't, that's fine too.

Be okay with failure, because failing is just learning the hard way, right?

Some of my closest, dearest, fiercely fabulous friends are friends because I was willing to get uncomfortable and chase after them.

Y'all know who you are. Have I told you lately how grateful I am for you?

Pour into your friendships, as the right ones will pour back into you.

We never know when God is putting someone in our path to be one of these people.

But if you're not willing to slow down, put down the phone (I said it), and receive the people around you, you'll miss some of life's greatest gifts.

> You will rarely be slapped by a God-wink. From what I've found, He rarely works like that. So be present, y'all, and heed my advice. When you take the time to slow down and give love, you open ourselves to receiving it.

The same can be said for new opportunities.

Whether it's new people, new places, new jobs, or new adventures, I promise you that nothing is guaranteed.

I know it won't always work out, but when it does, it's magical. Find the magic in your life.

Unapologetic Truth #26: The Final Unapologetic Truth

My biggest aspiration and "why" for this book was to enlighten you with my journey in hopes that it could empower you to become Unapologetically You in your own life.

But in addition to that, my second hope in sharing my story with you was a close runner-up. You ready for it?

Here's the corniest line yet; please know it's a miracle I made it this long before springing it on you, I believe so strongly in the **power of love**. Not the song, but the power of what we know love can be, 1 Corinthians 13: 4–8.

Every significant moment in my life, my biggest blessings, my proudest accomplishments, the greatest rewards, and the life-changing relationships I've been blessed with have all come from simple opportunities I've been presented to go out of my way to love on people.

Most have started out as nothing but interactions with strangers, but with intentionality, kindness, belief, and oftentimes a hug or two, I've loved my way into the lives of some pretty amazing people, moments, and opportunities.

These relationships have opened doors I didn't think possible. They even brought us together. God-winks.

I've felt how receiving love has transformed my life, I've seen how giving it has transformed the lives of others, and I know that it has the power to do the absolute unthinkable.

Love wins. Love never fails.

It's always worth looking and fighting for.

So I leave you with only the Biggest Hugs and Love.

I challenge you to go out into this world and be the light even in the darkness, pour love into the people around you even if it means you go on a few bad first dates, and live your life to the absolute fullest.

Be Unapologetic—why be anything but?

What's holding you back from embracing exactly who you were meant to be?

And just remember, I love you more.

• • •

Acknowledgments

A Moment for Gratitude

• • •

To Ryan Taft, thank you for naming this book before I wrote a word of it.

To my teachers, mentors, counselors, and unofficial fans, thank you for seeing things in me when I couldn't see them in myself. Thank you for choosing a life of servant leadership that's impact spans vastly beyond my story. You are the true heroes.

To my tribe, thank you for pouring yourself into me during all chapters of my life. Thank you for reading these pages before anyone else did. Thank you for believing in me whether I succeeded or failed. Thank you for loving me exactly as I am.

To my family, both blood and bonus, you've taught me so much and stood by me through it all. Thank you.

To my partner, lifeline, and very best friend—Eric, with our feet in the sand, you told me you'd bet on me any day (and this book was no exception) and for those moments, my unexpendable love for you grows even more. Thank you will never be enough.

To my girls, my ultimate "why." I fight for my very best self every day so that you can have exactly what you deserve, the very best version of me, and the very best mom by your side as you aspire to all you want to be. I love you the most.

• • •

Appendix

* * *

"Make a Difference"

There's an old man at my school
And his smile lights up the room
And his wrinkles
The everlasting lines
Tell the story of his time

There's a doctor down the street
And her mission is bittersweet
As she rescues another innocent life
She'll sleep better, another unforgettable fight

What do you do to make a difference?
How will you sacrifice?
Be a leader and a fighter
Make a difference and change a life

There's a soldier in my house
And his duty is restless now
As they all go to try to fight the fight
For our freedom, it's America's right

What do you do to make a difference?
How will you sacrifice?
Be a leader and a fighter
Make a difference and change a life

Look forward in the darkness
Hold your head high
There are heroes all amongst us
You can make wrong right

What do you do to make a difference?
How will you sacrifice?
Be a leader and a fighter
Make a difference and change a life

• • •

Notes

Notes

Notes

Notes

Notes

Notes

Notes

Notes

Notes

Notes